WITHDRAWN

John Tampion

Dangerous Plants

David & Charles
Newton Abbot · London · Vancouver

ISBN 0 7153 7375 7

Set in 11 on 12 pt Times
and printed in Great Britain
by Redwood Burn Limited, Trowbridge
for David & Charles (Publishers) Limited
Brunel House Newton Abbot Devon

Published in Canada
by Douglas David & Charles Limited
1875 Welch Street North Vancouver BC

Contents

1 The Problem and the Solution

Very early in his existence, if we may judge by all the records, man learned to distinguish harmful plants from edible ones. No doubt this was at first by trial and error. In many cases the association between eating a certain berry or plant and subsequent sickness, pain or death would be quite clear. Experience and verbal communication were the only means of gaining this important information, but everyone knew the plants.

Today, in the 'advanced' countries, this knowledge has unfortunately been lost by an overwhelming majority of families. True, the information *is* available from books and known to a few learned scientists, but that is of little use if it is your child who is being sick and crying out from pain. Nor is it any use if you, yourself, are lying on the bed in agony.

This book is intended for everybody: for the mother, in the hope that it may save her child's life; for the housewives and gardeners who handle plants; for the health-food and back-to-nature proponents; for the school teachers and educationists; perhaps even for the city doctor who has not previously considered the possible extent of the danger ensuing from many common or garden plants.

Dangerous plants are found all around us. In the home many potted plants and floral decorations are actually poisonous. Others may be harmful simply because of the allergies which they produce in particular members of the family. In the greenhouse and garden additional harmful species can be found, often originally imported from other countries and now much modified by the plant breeders' skill. Out in the fields, hedgerows and woods occur more dangerous plants to add to the list. Back in the kitchen still more dangers lurk in the food itself. This last hazard is not limited to those who have mistakenly collected as edible some poisonous wild plant.

Prevention is better than cure and in this case prevention means prior knowledge. Every man, woman and child should know and be able to recognise the dangerous plants which they are likely to come across. Young children frequently chew anything within reach. If the parents knew the dangers many accidents could be prevented. Accidental poisoning of older children and adults is usually due to faulty identification, often of wild plants which are mistaken for edible species.

The back-to-nature movement, with its worship of 'natural' food has led many townsfolk to seek out wild plants as a source of wholesome nourishment. Nothing is more dangerous than the ignorant disciple, armed only with word-of-mouth descriptions or the torn-out page of a magazine, loose in the countryside looking for free food. Sooner or later this leads, inevitably, to very unpleasant, if not lethal, consequences. Such people lack the basic country lore which enables a person to recognise one plant from another. The deadly *Amanita* toadstools, for example, can easily be confused with edible species. Hemlock has been mistaken for celery.

In a completely separate category is the deliberate consumption of plant material containing pharmacologically active ingredients to produce some desired effect. Often this starts with a group of so-called 'liberated' people. Someone reads of the effects of a certain plant in a newspaper or magazine, tries it out and then passes the great discovery to others, as the craze spreads. Such plants are often well-known (to scientists) as poisonous species with a range of serious side-effects. Frequently they can inflict permanent damage to the body or mind, destroying liver and kidney function or precipitating mental defects. Unfortunately, the mass media tend to sensationalise such outbreaks instead of presenting the grim facts from the doctors' casebooks. Excessive consumption of nutmeg, for example, to induce a 'high', can lead to prolonged hospitalisation and treatment extending over many months.

Why then are some plants poisonous and others edible? Even now, with all our scientific knowledge, we cannot be sure of the answer. Certainly they were not created by God as a punishment to man. Nor were poisonous plants created for his benefit (if taken in very small doses) as the Doctrine of Signatures might suggest with its theory that each plant was given a special appearance so that we would know which disease it could be used to treat. Most recent scientific studies, however, suggest that plants contain toxic ingredients to deter animals – in particular insects – from eating them.

Nearly all the poisonous substances found in plants belong to the category known to plant biochemists as 'secondary compounds'. This means that they are not substances essential to life itself. Only certain plants have developed particular secondary substances. Often, many plants in a single family will all possess a certain type of poisonous ingredient. The nightshade family, for example, is well known for its poisonous constituents. Yet, not every member of a 'poisonous plant family', nor even every part of a single 'poisonous plant' need actually contain the poisonous ingredient.

The explanation for this apparently random distribution of poisons must clearly be sought in the processes of evolution and natural selection. Nothing is produced in nature without a reason. Apart from the fungi, nearly all the plants mentioned in this book belong to the most advanced form of plant life – the flowering plants. Looking back to the fossil record we find that, at the time when various types of flower were first evolving, there was also an associated burst of evolution among the insects, with the formation of many previously unknown forms. The possession of poisonous ingredients gave certain plants a slight advantage in the struggle for existence.

6

Only many thousands of years later did man appear on the scene as a distinct species. It was his misfortune to discover that the Garden of Eden no longer existed! We can therefore forget any direct, causal, relationship between poisonous plants and man. Man's knowledge and his desire to understand, explain and exploit are the only links. At first this was no doubt a simple case of food supply and survival. Very soon other properties were noticed in the plants and a distinction of intent separated their use to kill from their use to cure. So began the noble science of medicine.

The pharmacological properties of such plants as the poppy, mandrake and henbane were well known thousands of years before the birth of Christ. We have written records of this, such as the Ebers Papyrus, dating from Ancient Egypt. The paths of herbal and 'qualified' medicine have since diverged so far as to make communication difficult between the two schools. Interestingly, many herbal cures which are once again becoming popular in the general 'back-to-nature' trend, can have quite serious effects if they are not applied with great care. Skin irritant and outrightly poisonous plants can produce worse symptoms than the 'diseases' they seek to cure.

Drug addiction is also as old as history. The hallucinogenic toadstool *Amanita muscaria* was worshipped as the narcotic god-plant Soma thousands of years ago by the ancient European invaders of north India. The 'flying mixtures' of witches are known to have contained belladonna and aconite, which cause delirium and affect the heart when rubbed onto the skin, producing the sensation of flying in the susceptible initiates. The peyote (mescal button) cult of the Native American Church boasts some quarter of a million adherents who sample the delights of the cactus *Lophophora williamsii*. Whole cultures have been founded on drug plants, wars fought and the future foretold under their influence. The upsurge of interest in the so-called 'meaning of life' has led many young people to experiment with drugs from plants on the false assumption that a chemical reaction in the nervous system can, somehow, lead to enlightenment. Cannabis, morning glory and nutmeg are just some of the highly dangerous plants handled by these foolish experimenters.

Crime is a natural companion to drug abuse. *Datura* has long been used to incapacitate victims, prior to robbery, in many eastern countries. In some places it is a favourite choice of prostitutes eager to gain more than their rightful payment. Conversely, it has been used as an aid to seduction, in which case women are usually on the receiving end of the treatment – so beware the incense smoke laced with stramonium! Actually, the plant is so dangerous that a fatal overdose is easily possible so that, like many so-called 'aphrodisiacs', the risks of overzealous use are very great.

Opium, or the drugs derived from it such as morphine and heroin, poses a serious problem because of the severe symptoms which occur when it is withdrawn. These are so unpleasant that criminal behaviour of any type whatsoever is regarded as better than being without a 'fix'. In the Western world much confusion exists between the really dangerous narcotics like opium and those like marihuana (*Cannabis*) where serious addiction is less common. The addictive tobacco, of course, is socially acceptable and a thoroughly respectable way for governments to raise money. Whatever the true status of *Cannabis* is as a drug of addiction the law-makers consider it to be a serious threat and it is certainly the hub of a network of criminal activities. The chief argument appears to lie in the ease of conversion from hemp (*Cannabis*), as it loses its effectiveness, to 'harder' narcotics. It is interesting to note that some investigators consider the 1951 outbreak of madness at Pont St Esprit in the south of France was caused by the accidental inclusion of hemp in the flour and not, as is usually concluded, a case of poisoning caused by the ergot fungus.

The most widespread outbreaks of serious poisoning due to plants are undoubtedly caused by the consumption of foods containing toxic natural substances. In the Middle Ages, ergotism caused by eating bread made from grain infected with the fungus *Claviceps purpurea* took a terrible toll of life, measured in tens of thousands of people. Two forms of the disease were produced, depending largely upon the vitamin content of the diet. In the most commonly described type the blood circulation was upset and burning sensations were felt in the limbs. At the time the cause was unknown, but people found that if they went on a pilgrimage to the shrine of St Anthony many were cured. So the poisoning became known as St Anthony's Fire. The cure was obviously due to the change in diet and consequent reduction in the intake of infected rye. People either recovered or died within a few days of arrival at the shrine. A distressing feature of ergotism is the blocking of the blood circulation to the tissues of the limbs, leading to their death and a shrivelling away of the affected limb. Fortunately such dangers are rarely encountered in the twentieth century.

Unfortunately, we cannot also say that lathyrism is a thing of the past. This condition was known in the time of Hippocrates and is described in Ancient Hindu literature. It is caused by eating the chick pea (*Lathyrus sativus*) and produces permanent crippling. Thousands of people, in particular in the poorest areas of India, have nothing else to eat and are forced to run the gauntlet of starvation or neurological damage. A relatively recent survey recorded over 20,000 cases in one district alone. The problem persists because the plant is hardy and survives where other, nutritionally better, plants cannot grow.

In all cases *knowledge* is the key to prevention. The purpose of this book is to present the necessary basic information. In Chapter 2 and the associated Appendix 1, I have attempted to describe or list all those plants which are likely to cause trouble in North America, the United Kingdom and many parts of Europe. Over a 100 plants are described, together with comments on where they are found and the symptoms produced. That is the section to read, study and learn.

Chapter 3 gives more general information concerning the nature of plant poisons and specific recommendations for treatment in the case of poisoning. For those with an immediate suspected case of plant poisoning I summarise here: 1 Keep any pieces of uneaten plant and vomited material; 2 If the patient is conscious make him sick at once and then seek medical advice, depending on the severity of the symptoms; 3 If the patient is unconscious seek medical help at once but *do not* attempt to make him sick.

Many people are sensitive to particular plants and may even develop severe symptoms from only casual contact. The establishment of cause and effect in this category of dangerous plant is often extremely difficult and may require many months of study. Allergies to plants form the basis of Chapter 4, and the associated Appendix 2.

Apparently wholesome, well-known, plant foodstuffs can be harmful for a variety of reasons. In Chapter 5 a number of ways in which danger can arise, even in the absence of contamination by toxic chemicals or micro-organisms, are described. Everybody concerned with food preparation or the selection of a good diet should particularly study this chapter.

This book was written to provide information on the dangers existing in plants. It should be read as a general source of information and then well-thumbed as a reference work. Take it round the house and check off the potted plants, into the greenhouse and garden for the cultivated flowers and shrubs, out into the fields and hedgerows and back into the kitchen to check the food. The author will consider his efforts worthwhile if it prevents just one poisoning, deters one reckless experiment or helps one person to detect an allergic response to a plant.

Let knowledge be your protection.

2 Plant Descriptions

The selection of the 100 plants fully described here has had to be on the basis of personal choice. Others, through lack of space, have been listed in Appendix 1, page 155. I hope that all readers will be inspired, at the very least, to seek out a picture and description of the species given in that appendix, to back up my necessary brevity.

The grouping of the plant descriptions has posed considerable problems since no single system is fully adequate. I have opted, therefore, for the one which I feel may be of most use to those using the book out of dire necessity. My major classification is into three categories: 1 Commonly cultivated; 2 Frequently growing wild; 3 Fungi.

As will be seen from the descriptions some plants, depending on where the reader lives, may be in either category 1 or 2. Within each major section the plants are arranged according to the part most likely to be eaten or cause trouble. Again this must be a somewhat arbitrary choice, arrived at mainly from the part concerned in recorded cases, so that inclusion in one particular subsection does not mean that other parts of the plant are harmless.

The botanically tidy classification by family, genus and species relationships has been discarded as useless, for practical purposes, as far as the average reader is concerned. In any case, such a system does not work even for a botanist, unless the flower is available and this is rarely the situation when a leaf or mature fruit has been consumed.

Illustrated Glossary of Terms Used in the Plant Descriptions

Accuracy is essential in identifying plants, but is almost impossible to achieve without the use of precise botanical terms which, although familiar to the scientist, are not normally used by the general public. This illustrated glossary is therefore necessary if the reader is to distinguish between different types of leaves, fruits etc and to recognise the various parts of flowers and fungi.

Leaves
Crisped   Curled
Cuneate   Wedge-shaped
Deciduous   Leaves fall off in the autumn

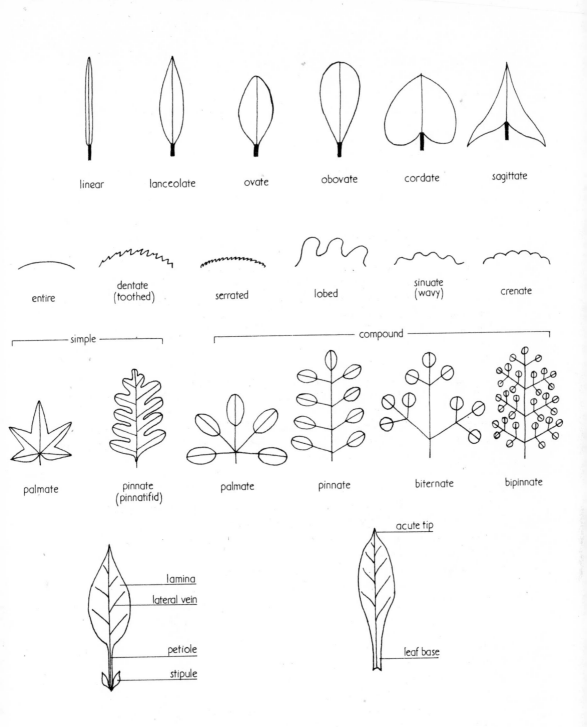

linear lanceolate ovate obovate cordate sagittate

entire dentate (toothed) serrated lobed sinuate (wavy) crenate

simple

palmate pinnate (pinnatifid)

compound

palmate pinnate biternate bipinnate

lamina
lateral vein
petiole
stipule

acute tip
leaf base

Fig. 1 Leaves

Evergreen	Green leaves persist over the winter
Glabrous	No hairs present
Incised	Cut into
Radical	Leaves which arise directly from a rootstock, not from an aerial stem
Rosette	Leaves clustered at ground level
Sessile	No stalk (petiole)
Truncate	Cut off straight across

Plants

Annual	Lasting only one year
Biennial	Lasting over two years (usually flowering only in second year)
Climbing	Any plant using an external support to raise itself above the ground. The term 'vine' is used for certain climbing plants
Cultivar	Cultivated form of a plant, recognised as distinct
Herb(aceous)	Non-woody plant or part of a plant
Lenticel	Pore in a corky layer (allowing gaseous exchange)
Node	Point at which leaves are attached to a stem
Perennial	Lasting several years
Spine	Sharply pointed outgrowth from a plant
Tendril	Modification of a leaf or stem which grips supports for climbing
Twining	Climbing by means of a stem which grows round supports
Whorled	Several parts (eg stems, leaves or flowers) arising in a ring around the stem

Flowers

Carpel	Female parts of a flower or one 'unit' of the female parts
Cluster	Undefined grouping of flowers
Female flowers	Flowers with carpels but no stamens
Filiform	Thread-like
Inflorescence	Group of flowers borne together
Perianth	Sepals and petals, or structure borne in their place
Zygomorphic	Irregular-shaped flower which can only be divided into two symmetrical halves along one plane

Fruits

Achene	Single-seeded, non-splitting fruit
Aril	Fleshy outgrowth from the basal region growing round a seed
Berry	Fleshy fruit, often containing many seeds
Capsule	Dry fruit, of more than one carpel, which splits open
Celled	Divided into distinct sections
Drupe	Fleshy fruit in which one or more seeds are present, each surrounded by a hard coat
Follicle	Dry fruit, splitting open along one side

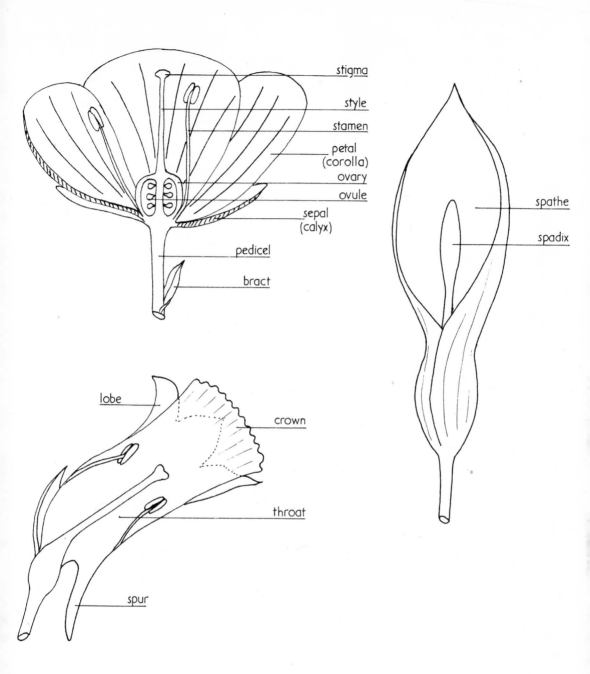

stigma
style
stamen
petal
(corolla)
ovary
ovule
sepal
(calyx)
pedicel
bract

spathe
spadix

lobe
crown
throat
spur

Fig. 2 Flowers

13

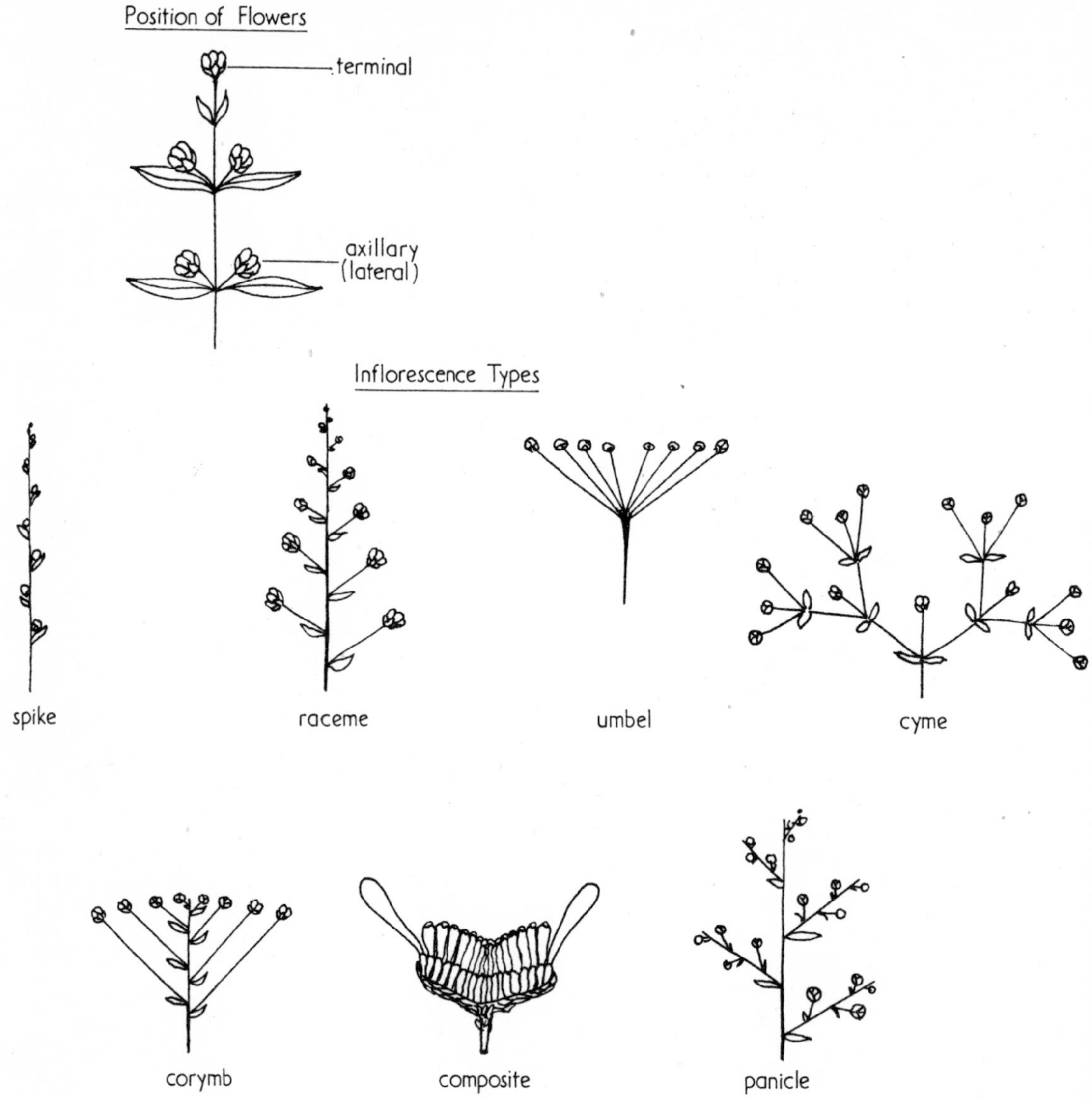

Position of Flowers

terminal

axillary
(lateral)

Inflorescence Types

spike

raceme

umbel

cyme

corymb

composite

panicle

Fig. 3 Flowers

14

Fruit	Ripe seeds and the structure surrounding them
Inflated	Swollen up
Mesocarp	Middle part of a fleshy fruit's covering
Pod	Dry fruit, splitting open along two sides
Valved	Segments splitting from a capsule

Underground Parts and Roots

Adventitious root	Root developing on a part of a plant (eg stem) other than a root
Anthropomorphic	Shaped like a human being
Bulb	Swollen leaves and base of a stem showing distinct layers when cut across
Corm	Swollen base of a stem, not consisting of layers
Rhizome	Swollen underground stem lasting more than one year
Rootstock(stock)	Swollen underground part of a plant
Taproot	Swollen main root
Tuber	Swollen underground portion of a root or stem

Fungi

| Flesh | Firm tissues, mainly in the cap |
| Viscid | Having thick, sticky liquid |

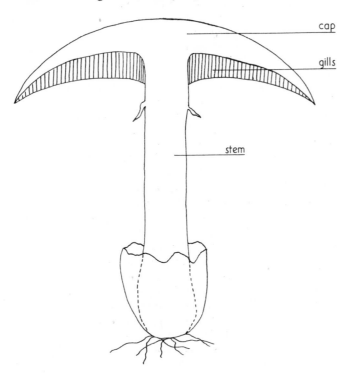

Fig. 4 Fungus

Dangerous Plants Commonly Cultivated

The page numbers (given in brackets) refer to the detailed plant descriptions.

Berries and Fruits

Dark blue, purple, brown, black:

CLIMBER	*Parthenocissus quinquefolia* (18)
BUSHY HERB, SHRUB OR TREE	*Cestrum nocturnum* (19)
	Lantana camara (20)
	Ligustrum vulgare (21)

Red, orange, dark pink:

SMALL HERB	*Convallaria majalis* (22)
CLIMBER	*Abrus precatorius* (23)
BUSHY HERB, SHRUB OR TREE	*Daphne mezereum* (24)

Yellow:

BUSHY HERB, SHRUB OR TREE	*Duranta repens* (25)
	Melia azedarach (26)
	Physalis peruviana (27)
	Solandra guttata (28)

Seeds

HERB	*Aconitum napellus* (29)
	Delphinium species (31)
	Digitalis purpurea (32)
	Hyoscyamus niger (33)
CLIMBER	*Cryptostegia grandiflora* (34)
	Ipomoea purpurea (35)
	Wisteria floribunda (36)
BUSHY HERB, SHRUB OR TREE	*Aesculus hippocastanum* (37)
	Aleurites fordii (38)
	Blighia sapida (39)
	Fagus sylvatica (40)
	Gymnocladus dioica (41)
	Hura crepitans (42)
	Jatropha curcas (43)
	Jatropha multifida (44)
	Laburnum anagyroides (45)
	Myristica fragrans (46)
	Poinciana gilliesii (47)
	Prunus serotina (48)
	Ricinus communis (49)
	Robinia psuedacacia (50)

Taxus baccata (51)
Thevetia peruviana (52)

Leaves or Stem

Dieffenbachia seguine (53)
Hydrangea macrophylla (54)
Nerium oleander (55)
Rheum rhaponticum (56)

Underground Parts

Colchicum autumnale (57)
Glòriosa superba (58)
Narcissus pseudo-narcissus (59)
Solanum tuberosum (60)

Contact with juice

Chelidonium majus (61)
Euphorbia pulcherrima (62)

Food Contaminant or Medicinal

Cannabis sativa (63)
Chenopodium ambrosioides (64)
Fagopyrum sagittatum (65)
Gelsemium sempervirens (66)
Papaver somniferum (67)
Podophyllum peltatum (68)

Units of Length

The metric system is used in descriptions but the following approximate conversions can be made:

To convert: mm to inches multiply by 0·04
cm to inches multiply by 0·4
metres to feet multiply by 3·3

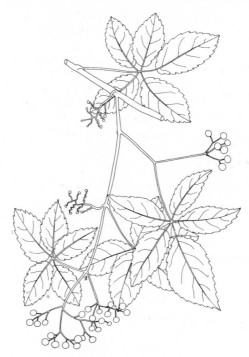

Parthenocissus quinquefolia

Parthenocissus quinquefolia (L.) Planch
(*Ampelopsis quinquefolia* Michx.)
Virginia Creeper/Woodbine
Vitaceae

Description Vigorous, high-climbing vine with branched (up to twelve) tendrils having adhesive tips. The five obovate leaflets are up to 15cm long and coarsely toothed. The small, greenish flowers are borne in a paniculate inflorescence. They are followed by small (about 8mm) bluish-black berries, each containing up to three seeds. Several cultivated forms occur, usually differing in leaf details and vigour.

Distribution and Habitat Wild forms occur in the US and several cultivated forms are found in Britain, Europe and North America. Commonly cultivated in gardens and around houses.

Dangers The berries are attractive to children and have been linked on circumstantial evidence to deaths – they have been proved toxic to some animals.

Related Plants About twelve species are described in this genus of tendril-climbers.

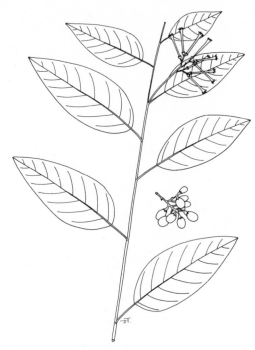

Cestrum nocturnum

Cestrum nocturnum L.
Night-blooming Jessamine
Solanaceae

Description This large shrub (up to 4m) has simple, entire elliptic to lance-olate leaves (up to 20cm long). The greenish-white flowers produce scent at night. They are trumpet-shaped (up to 2·5cm long) and are borne in clusters in the leaf axils. They are followed by small rather dry berries containing several seeds. The berries are purplish black (up to 1cm in diameter).

Distribution and Habitat Frequently grown in gardens in the southern US, or under glass elsewhere.

Dangers The symptoms of poisoning include nervous and muscular excite-ment, hallucinations, tachycardia (abnormal rapidity of heart-beat), saliva-tion, breathing difficulties and paralysis. Probable cause is an alkaloid, perhaps atropine.

Related Plants About 150 species are described in the genus. *C. diurnum* L. (day-blooming jessamine) is cultivated in southern US and may naturalise. Its flowers are day-scented and white and it is considered toxic. *C. parqui* L'Her (willow-leaved or green jessamine) is found wild in the southern US may also be cultivated and is toxic.

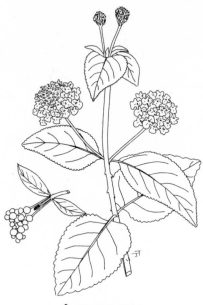

Lantana camara

Lantana camara L.

Lantana

Verbenaceae

Description Perennial herb or shrub up to 2m high with square stems bearing a few spines. The ovate, crenate/dentate leaves (up to 12·5cm) give off a strong odour when crushed. The small tubular flowers, varying from yellow to bright red, are borne in dense clusters at the end of a long stalk. They are followed by small (7mm diameter) blue-black fleshy, drupes containing one seed each.

Distribution and Habitat Cultivated as a shrub in southern US, a herbaceous plant and finally as a summer annual/greenhouse plant as it moves further north into Canada. It has escaped and naturalised in the southern US. Also sometimes cultivated in Europe and Britain.

Dangers The berries are attractive to children and have been instrumental in poisoning and deaths. Symptoms were those of gastrointestinal irritation with abdominal pain, diarrhoea, weakness, failure of the blood circulation and death in serious cases. These effects are ascribed to the polycyclic terpenoid Lantodene A. Jaundice and some degree of photosensitivity may also occur.

Related Plants *L. aculeata* L., *L. sellowiana* Link & Otto and *L. ovatifolia* Britton are described as equally toxic and all species of *Lantana* should be considered potentially dangerous.

20

Ligustrum vulgare

Ligustrum vulgare L.

Common privet

Oleaceae

Description Shrubby plant (up to 5m) with simple, entire, ovate/lanceolate leaves (up to about 6cm long). The small (up to 5mm) whitish, flowers are borne in pyramidal inflorescences and they develop to give clusters of blue-black, waxy berries which contain up to four seeds.

Distribution and Habitat Extensively cultivated in Europe and North America as a hedge plant or occasionally solitary. Often clipped to produce a dense growth. Native to Britain and Europe, often preferring calcareous soils.

Dangers Children have been poisoned by the attractive berries, although these usually only occur on untrimmed or neglected plants. Symptoms are those of gastric irritation with vomiting and purging, followed in severe cases by death. The active ingredient is the glycoside ligustrin.

Related Plants *L. lucidum* Ait. (glossy privet) and *L. japonicum* Thunb. and other species are also considered to have toxic berries. *L. ovalifolium* Hassk., with longer-persisting leaves is commonly used for hedging. About fifty species are known in the genus, as well as several cultivars, some yellow-leaved.

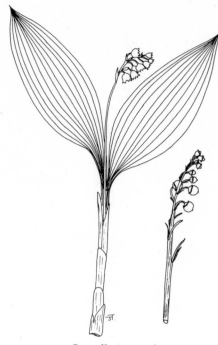

Convallaria majalis

Convallaria majalis L.
Lily of the valley
Liliaceae

Description A perennial creeping rootstock gives rise to pairs of simple, broadly ovate radical leaves (up to about 25cm long), the petiole of the lower clasping the upper. The flowering stalks are leafless and have a terminal, loose one-sided, raceme of drooping, white, bell-shaped flowers (up to 8mm) with an attractive scent. The fruit is a red globular berry, containing several seeds.

Distribution and Habitat Commonly cultivated, in shady places in gardens, throughout the UK, Europe and North America and occasionally escaping. Native to Britain and Europe.

Dangers The plants throughout contain cardiac glycosides (see page 129), called convallarin and convallamarin. Taken in small amounts the symptoms are abdominal pain and purging with a slowing and strengthening of the heartbeat. With larger amounts, greater nervous involvement giving mental disturbance, convulsions and perhaps death could occur. The plant is easily available to children who could be tempted by the bright berries or flower. It formerly had some folk-medicinal uses.

Related Plants Three species are recognised in the genus.

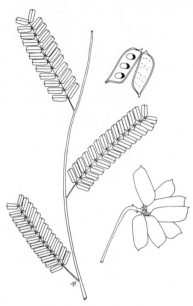

Abrus precatorius

Abrus precatorius L.
Rosary pea/Precatory bean
Leguminosae

Description A perennial climbing plant twining round trees up to 6m. The green to grey stems bear pinnate leaves with eight to fifteen leaflet pairs, each about 1·5cm long. The small red/purple flowers are borne in axillary racemes (up to 7·5cm long) and followed by a fine hairy pod (about 4cm long) containing many glossy jet black/scarlet ovoid seeds (about 1cm long or less).

Distribution and Habitat Originally a tropical plant now introduced into the southern US, and a weed of hedgerows and rough cultivated ground. Occasionally cultivated as an ornamental plant or for its seeds. Necklaces and trinkets made with the seeds were formerly common in North America, Britain and Europe. It is now banned in many places but may still be encountered.

Dangers The seeds are very toxic, less than one seed contains enough abrin to kill an adult. The symptoms are at first gastrointestinal, with purging and temperature fluctuations followed by incoordination and paralysis. Many different tissues are found to be damaged during post-mortem examinations. Growing plants, seeds and any objects containing the seeds should be considered highly dangerous and stringent measures taken to prevent children from having access to them.

Related Plants The family contains several other poisonous genera.

Daphne mezereum

Daphne mezereum L.
Spurge laurel/Mezereon
Thymelaeaceae

Description This small (up to about 1·5m) deciduous shrub bears simple, entire, broadly linear to obovate leaves (up to 7·5cm long).

The purple (white in some cultivars) fragrant flowers appear in sessile clusters of up to five, before the leaves, along the main branches. They have a tubular, coloured calyx (1·5cm) and no corolla.

The fruits are small (7·5mm) round drupes varying in colour from yellowish to bright scarlet, each containing a single seed.

Distribution and Habitat Commonly grown as an ornamental in gardens and used by flower arrangers in Europe, Britain and North America. Occasionally found in a naturalised state in some areas.

Dangers The fruit is attractive to children and a few have proved fatal. Other parts of the plant are also toxic. The juice of the plant is a primary irritant and produces burning and inflammation of the mouth and throat. Severe gastroenteritis occurs with vomiting and bloody diarrhoea. Weakness, stupor, renal damage with hematuria and convulsions may occur before death. Considered highly dangerous.

Related Plants Several other species, all considered dangerous, are grown as ornamentals and hybrids also exist. *D. laureola* L. has blue/black fruit and persistent leaves. *D. cneorum* L. has orange and *D. genkwa* Sieb. & Zucc. white fruits.

24

Duranta repens

Duranta repens L.
Golden dewdrop
Verbenaceae

Description Small tree or shrubby plant (up to 6m) with sometimes spiny, drooping branches. The roughly ovate leaves (up to 5cm long) are entire or have a somewhat toothed margin towards the tip. The flowers are borne in loose inflorescences up to 15cm long. The corolla is lilac, white or purplish, with a tubular portion and five terminal lobes. The yellow, globular juicy fruit (up to about 1cm in diameter) contains eight seeds and is enclosed in the persistent calyx whose lobes are closed to form a curved beak above the fruit. Some varieties have variegated leaves.

Distribution and Habitat Found in the open in southern Florida and sometimes cultivated elsewhere in greenhouses. Native to West Indies, South America and Key West.

Dangers Children are said to have been poisoned (some fatally) from eating the fruit. It contains a saponin-type poison which induces sleepiness, fever and convulsions.

Related Plants The genus contains about ten species.

Melia azedarach

Melia azedarach L.
Chinaberry tree/White cedar
Meliaceae

Description This small tree (up to about 15m) has large compound leaves with ovate/lanceolate leaflets (about 5cm long) having coarsely serrated margins. The purple flowers (2–5cm diameter) are borne in loose axillary panicles (up to 20cm long) and followed by small (up to 1·5cm) yellow, ovoid fruits containing a deeply ribbed stone. Several cultivated forms are known.

Distribution and Habitat Frequently planted in the southern US as an ornamental. Originally native to south-west Asia but naturalised in some parts of the southern US.

Dangers Children have died from eating the berries and adults from making a brew out of the leaves. A resinous poison is in the fruit pulp, but the amount may vary with the strain and growing conditions. The irritant activity of the plant is shown by vomiting and constipation or diarrhoea. Difficulty in breathing, weakening heart activity and nervous depression or excitement and paralysis may develop. Symptoms may occur up to a period of several hours and death may take place within a few days.

Related Plants *M. azedarach* var *umbraculiformis*, a horticultural form, is known as the Texas umbrella tree. The genus contains about twelve species.

26

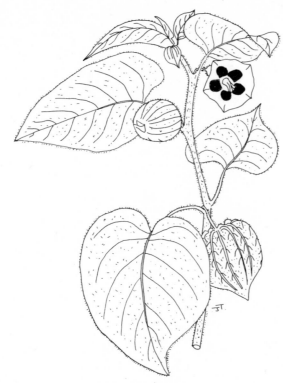

Physalis peruviana

Physalis peruviana L.
Ground-cherry/Cape-gooseberry/Poha
Solanaceae

Description The stout stems (up to 1m) bear ovate, cordate/truncate-based leaves up to 8cm long. The margins are toothed to the base. The flowers are expanded-bell-shaped (up to 1·5cm long). They are light yellow and have darker, purplish, blotches inside. The calyx becomes inflated after fertilisation to enclose the yellow, two-celled, globular fruit.

Distribution and Habitat Originally a tropical plant but commonly cultivated in the southern US and sometimes elsewhere in America and the UK.

Dangers The fruit is edible though rather sharp when ripe, but is considered poisonous when unripe. The symptoms are those of gastroenteritis. Some species of *Physalis* have sweeter, more glutinous berries and are preferred for eating.

Related Plants *P. longifolia* Nutt. is the ground-cherry. *P. alkekengi* L. (*P. franchetii*, Hort.) is the garden Chinese lantern-plant with coloured calyx bladders. The genus contains about 100 species.

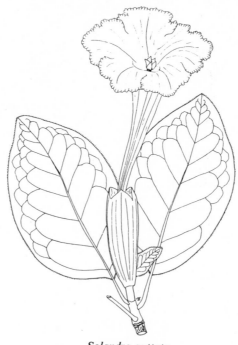

Solandra guttata

Solandra guttata Don.
Trumpet flower/Chalice vine
Solanaceae

Description A strong branching shrub climbing on supports. The leaves are oblong/elliptical (up to 15cm long), blunt or slightly pointed at the tip. The solitary yellow flowers are borne terminally on the stems. They are fragrant and funnel-shaped (up to 23cm long) with the tubular part protruding by several inches from the calyx (which is 8cm long). The expanded end has five wavy lobes and the throat bears five brownish ridges. The fruit is somewhat globular and yellowish, containing large smooth seeds.

Distribution and Habitat Commonly cultivated outdoors in the warmer parts of the US, and in greenhouses elsewhere in North America, Europe and Britain. Native to Mexico.

Dangers The plant contains solanine type alkaloids and may produce poisoning if eaten. Symptoms include dry throat, headache, weakness, fever, delirium, hallucinations and circulatory and respiratory failure. Deaths have occurred, even from chewing fragments of the flowers.

Related Plants Most of the six or so species of *Solandra* are considered toxic.

28

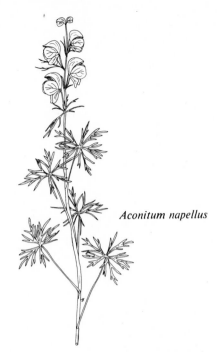

Aconitum napellus

Aconitum napellus L. (aggregate)
Monkshood/Aconite/Wolfsbane
Ranunculaceae

Description A blackish tuberous rootstock gives rise to several palmate leaves. The width of the deeply cut lobes is usually narrower in the wild forms of the plant and all forms may have additional subdivision and toothing of the lobes. When flowering, a tall (up to 1·5m) stem grows up carrying a raceme of zygomorphic five-membered flowers. The uppermost perianth segment forms a 'hood' over the others. Wild plants often have blue-mauve flowers but cultivated forms range from yellow, white and purple, dark purple to rich blue. Wild forms flower earlier than the garden ones. The ripe follicles contain many seeds.

Distribution and Habitat The plant occurs naturally in the north-temperate zones of Britain, Europe, Asia, and North America, usually preferring shady, moist places. Cultivated forms and species are widely grown outdoors in the north-temperate zone, for their attractive flowers.

Dangers Careless people have mistaken the tuberous 'roots' for horseradish or celery and the leaves for parsley. Children may eat leaves, flowers or seeds. First symptoms, showing within a few minutes, include tingling of the mouth, stomach and skin, restlessness, followed by slow pulse, incoordination and muscular weakness. Vomiting, diarrhoea, convulsions and death by respiratory or cardiac failure may follow in up to eight hours. Typically, the brain remains unaffected till the end. Considered very dangerous.

Related Plants Probably about 100 different species of *Aconitum* with several forms of some species. All probably poisonous. Several species and hybrids are commonly cultivated.

29

Delphinium ajacis

Delphinium species
Larkspur/Delphinium
Ranunculaceae

Description Since considerable difficulties exist in identifying the various species, which frequently hybridise between one another, only a general description will be given. A rhizomatous or single/clustered tuberous root-stock gives rise to an erect flowering stem of from about 0·25–2·5m height depending on species. Some are annuals, most perennial. The simple, stalked leaves are lobed (often deeply) into three to five major divisions and often many further subdivisions. The flowers are zygomorphic and spurred, borne in racemes or panicles and usually very attractive with coloured sepals as well as petals. The fruits consist of many-seeded follicles, one to three or more per flower.

Distribution and Habitat The various species occur all over the northern hemisphere including North America. Cultivated forms and species, many formed by hybridisation and selection, are very commonly grown in gardens for their attractive flowering stems.

Dangers The whole plant may contain various complex alkaloids, several of which have been fully characterised. There is considerable seasonal variation in alkaloid content but the seeds are usually considered to be highly toxic and are the part most likely to be eaten by children playing with the attractive ripening fruit-stalk. Fortunately the seeds drop out (or should obviously be removed) prior to use of the dried stems in indoor flower arrangements. The alkaloids act on the nervous system causing general weakness and eventual respiratory paralysis. Constipation, nausea and abdominal pain are common. Vomit may enter the lungs, due to general weakness, and cause respiratory difficulties.

Related Plants About 200 distinct species are recognised as well as numerous hybrids and cultivated forms. Although some are less toxic than others it is probably safest to consider all as potentially dangerous.

31

Digitalis purpurea

Digitalis purpurea L.
Foxglove
Scrophulariaceae

Description The erect, hairy, flowering stems may be up to 150cm high and are produced in the second year of growth from the original basal rosette. Occasionally the plant may perennate. The leaves are ovate/lanceolate with crenate margins and are hairy, particularly on the lower surface. The large (up to 5cm long) flowers are borne in terminal racemes of up to eighty flowers. They are usually pinkish–purple with darker spots inside but may also be overall paler, white or unspotted. The inflated capsule is slightly longer than the calyx, contains many tiny seeds and opens along the lines of its two cells.

Distribution and Habitat Native to Britain and Europe, in North America this plant has now spread from cultivation and is locally common in open land, roadsides and waste areas. Often abundant in clearings and after burning in light dry soils. Commonly grown in gardens.

Dangers Poisoning can result from eating any part of the plant or any material or drug derived from it. It contains about a dozen different cardiac glycosides and symptoms include abdominal pain, diarrhoea and nausea with strong nervous symptoms such as an increase in the strength of the heartbeat with a slowing of its rate, drowsiness or mental disturbance and even tremors and convulsions. Death may occur.

Related Plants Several horticultural cultivars and species are in cultivation and all should be considered dangerous. About twenty species are described in the genus.

Hyoscyamus niger

Hyoscyamus niger L.
Henbane/Black henbane
Solanaceae

Description A biennial or annual, erect, hairy herb up to 1m high, with coarsely toothed, oblong ovate leaves (up to 20cm). The bell-shaped flowers have a yellow, usually purple-veined corolla (up to 3cm diameter) and purple anthers. Mostly they occur more or less sessile in the leaf axils or more crowded towards the stem apex. After fertilisation the calyx continues growing around the fruit as a five-pointed cover. The globular capsule (up to 20mm) opens by a circular lid mechanism.

Distribution and Habitat Native to Britain and Europe the plant has been widely grown as a medicinal herb and escaped in some places in Canada and the US. Usually prefers dryish, disturbed soils such as roadsides and waste places.

Dangers Although many cases of poisoning have occurred, especially of children, its comparative rarity makes such cases infrequent now. The alkaloids present are mainly hyoscyamine with some hyoscine and atropine. The symptoms include delirium, visual disturbance, rapid weak heartbeat, convulsions, coma, and may end in death. Some authorities suggest its poisoning can be distinguished, by its excessive salivation, from that caused by *Atropa* or *Datura*.

Related Plants Some eight species are recognised in the genus. The family contains many other poisonous genera.

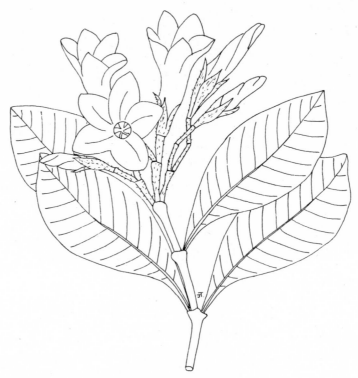

Cryptostegia grandiflora

Cryptostegia grandiflora R. Bv.
Rubber-vine/Pink allamanda
Asclepiadaceae

Description A woody vine with thick stems and milky juice. The shiny glabrous opposite leaves are oblong (up to 10 × 5cm). The large (up to 7·5cm across) flowers are borne in terminal clusters. They have a leafy calyx (1·5cm long) and a corolla with a short tube and expanded bell-like outer parts. Attached to the corolla is a 'crown' of five 'scales' each deeply split into two filiform segments. The fruit is a sharply angled follicle (up to 10cm long).

Distribution and Habitat Grown as an ornamental in warmer parts of the US it has naturalised in some places in Florida and can be found in waste places and by roads. Native to Africa.

Dangers Severe gastroenteritis with pain, vomiting and diarrhoea has resulted in death after eating this plant's seeds.

Related Plants Three species are recognised in this genus of tropical plants. The family contains over 2,000 species in some 220 genera.

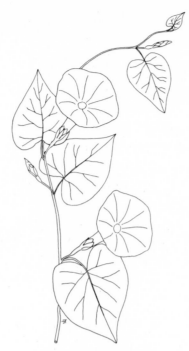

Ipomoea purpurea

Ipomoea purpurea Lam.

Morning glory

Convolvulaceae

Description A tall, twining annual plant with hairy stems. The leaves are entire and broadly ovate/cordate (up to 12cm long) The purplish/bluish funnel-shaped flowers (up to 7·5cm long) are borne in groups of one to five in the leaf axils. The fruit is a capsule, splitting to reveal the seeds. Many cultivated forms are described.

Distribution and Habitat Commonly cultivated throughout North America, Europe and Britain, often under greenhouse conditions. Native to tropical America and capable of some degree of establishment in the warmer areas.

Dangers The major active substance found, for example, in the seeds which are often self-administered, is d-lysergic acid amide, a well-known hallucin-ogen. It has been held responsible for deaths linked to continuing psycho-logical disturbances over a period of days or weeks. Its effects are unpredict-able and last for a number of hours. If pleasant, they may include heightened (distorted) perception of vision, smell and sound but are frequently very unpleasant and cause permanent damage to the mind.

Related Plants Over 400 species are described in the genus.

Wisteria floribunda

Wisteria floribunda DC.
Japanese wisteria
Leguminosae

Description Woody shrub often growing as a vine climbing (tied) on walls. Young branches twining. The pinnate leaves have up to nineteen ovate leaflets up to 7·5cm long.

The flowers (shades from white, pink and blue to purple depending on variety) are up to 2cm long and borne in long, hanging racemes (up to 45cm long). The pod is finely hairy (up to 15cm long). Some cultivated varieties have longer racemes and longer leaves. Double forms are known.

Distribution and Habitat Commonly cultivated throughout North America, Europe and Britain. Native to Japan.

Dangers Children have been poisoned by eating pods and seeds. The symptoms are those of gastroenteritis, with abdominal pain, vomiting and diarrhoea. In severe cases serious dehydration occurred. It is thought that eating only a few seeds can produce poisoning.

Related Plants The commonly cultivated *W. sinensis* (Chinese wisteria) with blue/violet flowers is also considered toxic, as well as the other seven species in the genus.

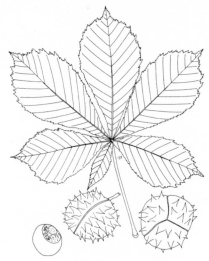

Aesculus hippocastanum

Aesculus hippocastanum L.
Horse chestnut
Hippocastanaceae

Description Stout tree (up to 25m) with leaves having a long petiole and five to seven palmate divisions. Each leaflet (up to 20cm) broadly obovate with an irregular serrated margin. The showy upright panicles contain white flowers (up to 2cm) with basal pink spots to the four petals. The well-known, shiny brown, seeds (conkers) are contained in the green, prickly fruit coat (up to 6cm in diameter).

Distribution and Habitat Commonly planted in Europe, Britain and America for ornamental use in parks and gardens but capable of naturalising from seed. Native to Greece and Albania.

Dangers Children collect the fruit to play 'conkers' and younger ones may consume them with fatal results due to the presence of the glycoside aesculin · which yields a toxic coumarin derivative on hydrolysis. Vomiting and diarrhoea are common symptoms.

Related Plants The genus has about twenty-five species. Several commercial cultivars and hybrids are available; some doubles, which do not produce seeds, can be grown as ornamentals. *A. californica* (Spach) Nutt., the California buckeye, is a small tree of drier places in the US and its pollen is thought to be toxic to bees and to give rise to toxic honey. *A. pavia* L. (red buckeye), *A. glabra* Willd. (Ohio buckeye) and *A. octandra* Marsh (sweet buckeye) as well as other species, should be considered potentially dangerous.

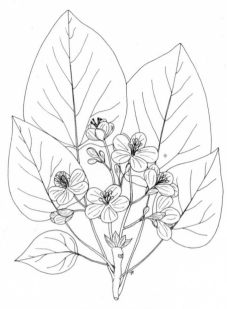

Aleurites fordii

Aleurites fordii Hemsl.
Tung-oil tree
Euphorbiaceae

Description The rather thick branches of this small tree are frequently borne in relatively regular whirls. The palmately veined simple leaves are up to 25cm long. The large (5–8cm diameter) fruit is at first green, ripening to brown. It contains from three to seven white-fleshed seeds.

Distribution and Habitat Native to Asia, it has been widely planted in America (especially in the Gulf Coast) for oil production and shade.

Dangers The large nuts are attractive and when opened have sometimes been mistaken for Brazil nuts. One seed can cause severe symptoms of vomiting, gastroenteritis with abdominal pain and diarrhoea, leading to exhaustion after a few hours. Shock, dehydration and respiratory depression with cyanosis (blueness of the skin) may develop prior to death. At least three toxic substances are present. One is destroyed by heating and sometimes called a 'saponin' or a 'phytotoxin'. The other two are stable to heating and are chemically related but have not been fully identified. Considered a highly dangerous plant. The sap, leaves and fruit can also cause injury. Symptoms may sometimes be delayed for up to several days.

Related Plants Two or three closely related species are often grown for oil or as ornamentals, but are sometimes considered rather less toxic than *A. fordii*. The raw seed of *A. moluccana* (Kukui) causes vomiting and purging.

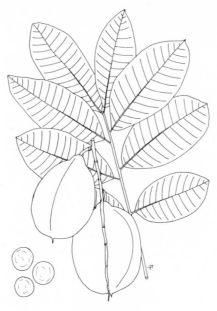

Blighia sapida

Blighia sapida Koenig
Akee
Sapindaceae

Description This small tree has pinnate leaves. The flowers are borne in axillary racemes with five petals each having scales on the inner side. The fruit is a capsule with thick walls. Several crops of fruit may be obtained in one year. The leathery skin of each fruit splits at maturity to reveal three chambers, each containing a large black seed stuck into an oily, light, whitish aril.

Distribution and Habitat Often cultivated in tropical regions and southern Florida for its fruit, although native to Africa.

Dangers Only the naturally ripened arils of opened, fertilised fruits are considered edible. Unripe, over-ripe or otherwise abnormal arils, seeds and fruit walls are considered toxic due to hypoglycaemic agents which deplete the body-sugar reserves and the blood-sugar level. Violent vomiting, quiet periods and finally coma and death commonly occur in children, particularly undernourished ones. Although the aril is normally cooked this may not inactivate all the toxic ingredients.

Related Plants Only one species is described for this genus but the family contains over a 1,000 species in about 125 genera.

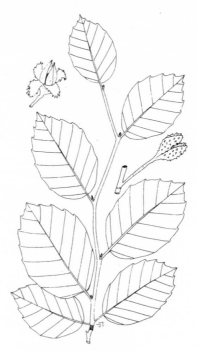

Fagus sylvatica

Fagus sylvatica L.
European beech
Fagaceae

Description Large tree (up to 30m or more) with smooth grey bark and simple entire, ovate leaves (up to 9cm), slightly sinuate and with a few silky hairs on the veins. The inconspicuous axillary female flowers are wind pollinated (male flowers in catkins) and are followed by a tough cover of prickly segments which spread to reveal the one or two large (up to 1·8mm) three-angled brown seeds.

Distribution and Habitat Native to parts of Britain and Europe and commonly planted there and elsewhere, including North America. Preferring chalk and soft limestone and well-drained light soils.

Dangers The seeds contain a poisonous saponin-type substance which can cause severe gastroenteritis with abdominal pain, diarrhoea and nausea. Some people can consume them with little effect.

Related Plants *F. grandiflora* Ehrh. is the American beech, existing in several, frequently cultivated varieties. Several varieties of *F. sylvatica* also exist, often with varying leaf characters.

Gymnocladus dioica

Gymnocladus dioica Koch.

Kentucky coffee tree

Leguminosae

Description Tall (up to 25m) much-branched tree with twice pinnate leaves up to 1m long. The leaflets are ovate and entire. The flowers are greenish-white, up to 1cm long; the females in racemes 10cm long and the males in 30cm ones. The fruit is a brown, flattened pod up to 15cm long containing several large (up to 2·5cm) flattened seeds.

Distribution and Habitat Native to eastern parts of the US and occasionally cultivated in other places.

Dangers The plant has been mistaken for the Gleditsia (honey locust) and its fruits eaten in error. They probably contain an alkaloid. Symptoms of poisoning are gastrointestinal irritation followed by a depressant action on the nervous system, simulating that caused by narcotics.

Related Plants The genus contains two species.

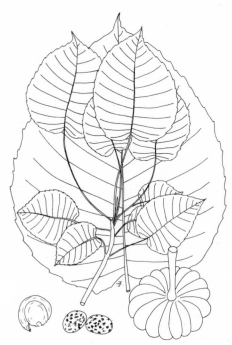

Hura crepitans

Hura crepitans L.
Sandbox tree
Euphorbiaceae

Description A tree (up to 20m) with a spiny trunk bearing simple, broadly ovate, pointed leaves (up to 22cm long), softly hairy on the underside. The flowers are dark-red, the female ones being in the form of a cap (2cm diameter) with a toothed edge. The fruit is woody (up to 10cm across and ribbed). It splits violently when ripe and throws the thin, flattened mottled-brown seeds (about 2cm across) a distance of many metres.

Distribution and Habitat Although really a tropical species this tree has been planted in the southern US.

Dangers Two or three seeds produce severe vomiting and purging when eaten. Some individuals develop a severe contact irritation on touching the plant; which is unfortunate as the woody fruit is occasionally used to make jewellery. As well as the substance causing digestive distress the plant is thought to contain a possible phytotoxin. Delirium, collapse and death may occur.

Related Plants The genus contains several other poisonous species and the family is well-known for its toxic sap.

Jatropha curcas

Jatropha curcas L.
Barbados nut/Curcas bean/Physic nut
Euphorbiaceae

Description This rank annual shrub or short-lived tree may reach 5m in height. Its thick, green stems bear large (about 15cm wide) cordate leaves with irregular or three- to five-lobed margins. The small, inconspicuous, yellow, one-sex, flowers produce an ovoid capsular fruit with three sections. At first green and fleshy it dries to a dark colour, containing two or three large (2cm) black seeds.

Distribution and Habitat Although a tropical plant it is commonly cultivated in the southern US as an ornamental hedge or shrub, praised for its rapid growth.

Dangers Eating the seeds or overdosing with the purgative oil can lead to gastroenteritis, vomiting and diarrhoea. The throat feels a burning sensation. Toxicity varies, possibly depending on the strain of plant; in some cases a few seeds, in others up to fifty, may be needed to produce severe symptoms. Apart from the oil itself a phytotoxin may be present in the seeds. Muscular cramps, dizziness and deafness may occur. Deaths of children have been recorded.

Related Plants *J. stimuloca* Michx. (bull or spurge nettle) causes painful or even severe skin irritation from its spiny hairs which carry an irritant fluid. Other species of *Jatropha* should be considered potentially dangerous. *J. multifida* is considered separately on page 44.

43

Jatropha multifida

Jatropha multifida L.
Coral plant/Physic nut
Euphorbiaceae

Description A small shrub (up to 2·5m) bearing nine- to eleven-lobed palmate leaves some 10 to 20cm wide. The leaf lobes may be entire or incised. The small, uni-sexual flowers give rise to yellow fruits which, although three-sectioned, remain closed as they ripen.

Distribution and Habitat Commonly cultivated in the US, but native only to the extreme south.

Dangers The yellow fruits are attractive to children and have frequently been eaten by them producing severe gastroenteritis, vomiting and diarrhoea. A burning feeling occurs in the mouth and throat. A phytotoxin is probably responsible for some of the symptoms, in addition to the purgative Jatropha oil. Muscular cramps, dizziness and deafness may occur. Deaths of children have been recorded.

Related Plants *J. gossypifolia* L. (bellyache bush) causes similar symptoms. *J. curcas* is mentioned separately on page 43.

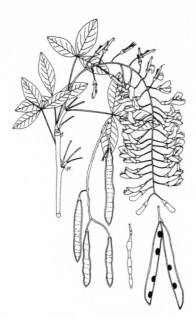

Laburnum anagyroides

Laburnum anagyroides Medic.
(*Cytisus laburnum* L.)
Laburnum/Golden rain
Leguminosae

Description Small tree or shrub (up to 10m), the twigs with close-pressed hairs and bearing trifoliate long-petioled (up to 8cm) leaves. The ovate leaflets are up to 8cm long. The yellow-lipped flowers (2cm long) are in long hanging racemes. Followed by pods (up to 5cm long) containing up to eight dark-brown, kidney-shaped seeds. The pods may remain attached and dried on the plant over the winter. The pods bulge distinctly over the seeds and burst open suddenly as they dry out. Some cultivated forms have yellow leaves.

Distribution and Habitat Commonly cultivated in North America and Britain for its flowers, but native only to central and southern Europe. Sometimes almost naturalised in waste, bushy places. Very common in gardens and parks.

Dangers The pods and seeds are attractive to children and have been fatal. Vomiting is common, with nervous symptoms such as excitement and inco-ordination. Convulsions, coma and death due to asphyxia may occur. Usually considered highly dangerous due to its very common occurrence in gardens and parks.

Related Plants Two species are described in the genus.

45

Myristica fragrans

Myristica fragrans Houtt.
Nutmeg
Myristicaceae

Description A tree with oval or oblong lanceolate leaves (up to 12cm long). The small flowers are borne in axillary clusters and are followed by a hanging globular/pearshaped (up to 5cm long) yellowish-red fruit. This splits into two valves to disclose a red aril (the mace) around the hard-shelled nutmeg.

Distribution and Habitat Native to Molucca, the plant is occasionally cultivated under glass. The seeds (nutmegs) and mace are readily obtainable in stores, everywhere, for culinary use as flavouring when ground.

Dangers Harmless in normal use, the dried seed kernel is sometimes ground and self-administered in large amount (more than one nutmeg) for medical or hallucinogenic reasons. Symptoms include numbness, dizziness and nausea. Visual and auditory distortions occur, sometimes described as pleasant. Prolonged sleep often occurs. Recovery may take some days. Deaths have occurred with liver and kidney damage.

Related Plants About eighty species are described in the genus, all from India, Australia or the Pacific Islands.

46

Poinciana gilliesii

Poinciana gilliesii Hook (*Caesalpinia gilliesii*)

Poinciana/Bird of paradise

Leguminosae

Description Shrub, sometimes a straggling climber or small tree. Leaves compound consisting of many pinnae with the leaflets linear/oblong (up to 12 × 4mm), usually with small black spots near the margins on lower side.

The large light-yellow flowers with red stamens up to 12cm long are borne in terminal racemes. They are followed by green pods (10cm × 2cm) containing the seeds.

Distribution and Habitat Cultivated outdoors in southern US, or elsewhere as a pot-plant, but native to South America.

Dangers The green pods with seeds cause severe gastrointestinal irritation with vomiting and diarrhoea. Children may be attracted to them but usually recover within a day of eating a few pods.

Related Plants A number of species are described in this genus of tropical and sub-tropical plants.

Prunus serotina

Prunus serotina Ehrh.
Wild black cherry
Rosaceae

Description A tree (up to 30m) with broadly lanceolate, serrate-margined leaves (blades up to 12cm) held stiff at maturity.

The white/pink flowers (about 6mm across) with five spreading petals are borne in racemes (up to 15cm long) on the current season's growth, and followed by globose, black (1cm diameter) fleshy fruits containing a single, hard stone and only a thin fleshy portion.

Distribution and Habitat Found in woods and hedges in the eastern US and Canada. Sometimes planted there and elsewhere for ornament or shade.

Dangers Children have been poisoned and died from eating the kernels which contain a cyanogenetic glycoside. The leaves are also toxic. The amount of other food eaten greatly influences the amount of cyanide absorbed. In small amounts the blood may remain red even in the veins, due to upsetting of the normal use of oxygen by the body tissues. In larger amounts a short period of rapid breathing is followed by collapse and death.

Related Plants The fruit stones of nearly all species of *Prunus* are considered toxic – including many with edible fruits such as apricot (*P. armeniaca* L.), peach (*P. persica* Batsch.), as well as wild cherry – due to the presence of cyanide producing glycosides. They should never be eaten like nuts. The bitter almond (*P. amygdalus* Batsch) is well-known to be toxic, as also is the cherry laurel (*P. laurocerasus* L.) The genus contains about 200 species.

48

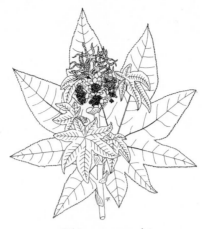

Ricinus communis

Ricinus communis L.
Castor bean/Palma christi
Euphorbiaceae

Description An annual growing to 2·5m with up to twelve lobes to the long stalked leaves. May also grow as a herbaceous tree up to 13m. Leaves may be up to 1m across.

The female flowers grow in erect panicles (up to 70cm long) occurring on the lower part of the plant. They are followed by a smooth or spiny capsule (up to 2·5cm long) containing seeds with variable brownish mottling on a whitish background. A number of cultivated forms are recognised, varying in foliage, capsule and seed characteristics.

Distribution and Habitat The plant needs a long growing season and is cultivated as a crop in California and southern US. Elsewhere in Europe and North America where the seed's oil is not required, it is often grown as an ornamental, indoors or in the greenhouse if necessary, usually using selected horticultural strains.

Dangers The whole plant (but not the oil prepared from the seeds) is poisonous. The seeds are extremely poisonous due to the presence of the phytotoxin ricin, which is amongst the most toxic substances known. As few as two seeds can prove serious or even fatal. Possible allergenic reactions of great severity have occurred with a single seed. A burning sensation in mouth and throat is followed, some hours or more later, by signs of gastroenteritis, diarrhoea, abdominal pain and weakness of body and pulse. The digestive tract shows hemorrhages and the liver and kidneys are damaged. Chewing castor beans as a laxative has proved fatal. Heating can inactivate the poison.

Related Plants Only one (very variable) species is described in this genus.

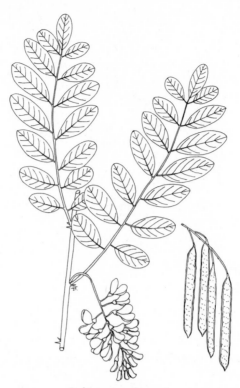
Robinia pseudoacacia

· *Robinia pseudoacacia* L.
Black locust/Acacia
Leguminosae

Description Slender trunked deciduous tree (to 25m) with stipular thorns on the young branches. Leaves pinnate (three to ten pairs) with entire elliptical leaflets. The white or pink scented flowers are borne in long hanging racemes (up to 20cm long) followed by a persistent, flattened legume pod containing many seeds.

Distribution and Habitat Native to eastern and central US and extending into south Canada, forming dense stands. Sometimes grown for timber or as an ornamental elsewhere in America and in Europe and Britain.

Dangers Children have been poisoned by the seeds and all parts of the plant are probably poisonous due to the presence of a toxin 'robin' and a glycoside 'robitin'. Symptoms include vomiting, diarrhoea weakness, dilated pupils, weak irregular pulse and breathing difficulties.

Related Plants Twenty species are described from North America.

50

Taxus baccata

Taxus baccata L.
English yew
Taxaceae

Description A shrubby or small tree, evergreen, with dark-green upper and paler lower-surfaced, narrow, linear leaves of up to about 2cm length. The leaves are carried in two rows, spreading laterally from the stems. Normally the plant is either male or female only. The ovules arise singly and are at first inconspicuous, but after fertilisation a bright pink-red, fleshy aril grows up around the seed. There is only a single, large (about 6mm long) oval, olive-brown seed per fruit.

Distribution and Habitat The plant occurs naturally in Europe and in the mountains of some Mediterranean countries, stretching into Asia and north Africa. Commonly found in America where (as elsewhere) it is used as an ornamental for hedging. It is tolerant of shade and often prefers calcareous soils.

Dangers The fleshy arils are considered quite safe but the seeds within them can contain dangerous levels of poison and may cause problems with children. Foliage and stems are also poisonous. The alkaloids in this plant slow the heart rate and, if taken in sufficiently large amounts, will stop it completely. Less severe cases may show collapse with trembling and some diarrhoea or general gastroenteritis. Potentially dangerous because of its bright fruit and frequent cultivation.

Related Plants Probably about seven species of *Taxus*. Some commonly cultivated, others native to the US and Canada. Possibly all toxic but most cases arise from the ornamentals *T. baccata* or *T. cuspidata*.

51

Thevetia peruviana

Thevetia peruviana Schum.
(*Thevetia nereifolia* Juss)
Yellow oleander/Be-still tree
Apocynaceae

Description Small tree/shrub (up to about 10m high) bearing linear, pointed leaves (up to 15cm long) with dark-green upper and lighter lower surface, the margins rolled. The large (7·5cm long) orange or yellow, tubular flowers are borne in clusters at the branch tips. The roughly triangular fruit has at first an outer yellowish-red fleshy portion ripening to black. The stony inner part usually contains two seeds.

Distribution and Habitat Cultivated as an outdoor ornamental in the southern US but originally native to tropical America. Occasionally grown under glass elsewhere.

Dangers All parts of the plant are poisonous due to cardiac glycosides such as thevetin. People have died from misusing the plant in native medicines, and children from eating the kernels, only one of which may be sufficient to be fatal. The pulse is slow and weak, vomiting and gastroenteritis may occur. Cardiac abnormalities follow and death due to cardiac failure.

Related Plants The genus contains about ten species, all native to tropical America.

52

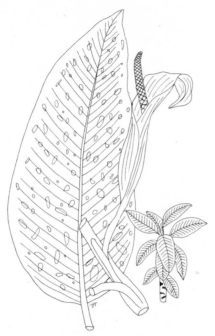

Dieffenbachia seguine

Dieffenbachia seguine Schott.
Dumbcane
Araceae

Description The green stems (up to 2m) bear large, oblong, entire leaves which may vary from mottled shades of white through yellow to completely green, depending on the cultivar. When the leaves fall they leave distinct leaf scars which ring the stem. A persistent spathe is formed with a lower curled portion around the female flowers and an upper narrow trough-shaped blade with the upper part of the spadix reaching almost to its tips.

Distribution and Habitat Hardy outdoors in southern US and extensively cultivated in greenhouses elsewhere in North America, Europe and Britain. Originally from South America and the West Indies.

Dangers Biting or chewing the stem of this plant results in burning sensations and irritation of the mouth, lips and tongue. Pronounced swelling restricts tongue movement, swallowing and breathing for up to several days. This effect is said to be due to fine crystals of calcium oxalate, but probably also involves some other toxic substance as well.

Related Plants The related genera of *Alocasia*, *Caladium* and *Xanthosoma* also contain irritant juices. *D. picta* has similar properties.

Hydrangea macrophylla

Hydrangea macrophylla Ser.
(*Hydrangea hortensis* Smith)
Hydrangea
Saxifragaceae

Description A stiff, much-branched shrub (up to 4m) with broadly ovate leaves (up to 15cm long) with coarsely toothed margins. The flowers are white, pink or blue and are borne in dense flat or roundish cymes. The calyx is expanded and attractive. The flowers are persistent for several months and in some cultivated varieties may be entirely sterile.

Distribution and Habitat Commonly grown outdoors or in pots as an ornamental throughout North America, Europe and Britain. Originally native to Japan.

Dangers The plant may contain cyanogenetic glycosides and has been responsible for poisoning when the buds have been added, in error, to a salad. The symptoms were of gastroenteritis type with abdominal pain, nausea and diarrhoea.

Related Plants *H. quercifolia* Batr. from south-eastern US and *H. arborescens* L. from the eastern US are found wild, but may also be cultivated elsewhere. Some eighty species are described in the genus.

Nerium oleander

Nerium oleander L.

Oleander

Apocynaceae

Description An evergreen shrub (up to about 7m high) with entire, broadly lanceolate, leathery leaves (up to 30cm long) each being sharply pointed. They are dark-green above, paler below. The white, pink or purplish flowers (up to 7·5cm across) are produced in large clusters. Some double-flowered forms are cultivated. The fruit is a hanging pod (up to 17cm long).

Distribution and Habitat Native to the Mediterranean region it is commonly cultivated outdoors in warmer parts of Europe and North America and as a pot-plant elsewhere.

Dangers All parts of the plant are highly toxic. Eating a single leaf or even eating meat skewered during cooking with oleander has been recorded as deadly. Cardiac glycosides (oleandroside and nerioside) have been isolated. Severe gastroenteritis, with dizziness, drowsiness, increased pulse rate, vomiting, abdominal pain and other miscellaneous symptoms, are followed by an irregular and weakened heartbeat, breathing difficulties, coma and eventually death. Symptoms commence in a few hours and death occurs usually within twenty-four hours.

Related Plants *N. indicum* Mill., of similar appearance, has also caused deaths although its active ingredients may be somewhat different.

Rheum rhaponticum

Rheum rhaponticum L.

Rhubarb

Polygonaceae

Description A stout fleshy, rootstock produces several large, roughly cordate, green leaves (up to 1·3m) each with a long stout petiole, green to bright red in colour. The leaves are almost all radical and often somewhat crinkled. The flowers occur in dense panicles up to 2m tall, borne on a hollow, erect, somewhat branching, stem. The greenish-white flowers are borne on slender pedicels and followed by a winged, roughly cordate fruit (about 1cm long).

Distribution and Habitat Commonly cultivated as a food plant for its edible petioles in Britain, Europe and North America. The original plant was probably from Siberia but extensive domestication and selection have now occurred.

Dangers The leaf blades contain dangerous quantities of oxalic acid and soluble oxalates and have caused deaths when eaten as a vegetable, even when small quantities were consumed. Vomiting, fluctuating abdominal pains and weakness precede death. Blood clotting is reduced, probably due to combination with plasma calcium to form oxalates. As a common garden plant the dangers cannot be over emphasised.

Related Plants *R. officinale* (medicinal rhubarb) has similar properties. The related genus *Rumex* is toxic to animals because of its oxalate content.

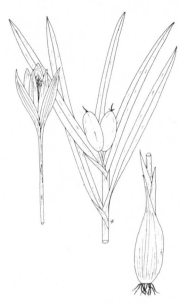

Colchicum autumnale

Colchicum autumnale L.
Autumn crocus/Meadow saffron
Liliaceae

Description In spring the corm (up to 5cm), covered in brown outer scales gives rise to several large, linear (up to 4 × 30cm) leaves. These die back before the white or purplish flowers are formed. These have a predominantly tubular perianth (up to 20cm long) with terminal lobes of about 4cm. The flower stalk elongates during the fruiting period, which is complete in the spring. The fruit is ovoid (up to 5cm), splits along the lines of the three ovaries, and contains many seeds.

Distribution and Habitat Native to Europe and Great Britain and cultivated there and in North America, sometimes naturalising. It prefers damp woods and meadows on non-acid soils.

Dangers All parts of the plant are poisonous due to alkaloids such as colchicine. The symptoms are mainly those of gastrointestinal irritation, with abdominal pain and diarrhoea. Muscular weakness, breathing difficulties and occasionally coma, convulsions and respiratory failure may occur. The toxins can pass in the milk of animals that have eaten *Colchicum* and can accumulate during slow ingestion to reach a toxic level.

Related Plants Some sixty-five species are recognised as well as several garden forms and selections.

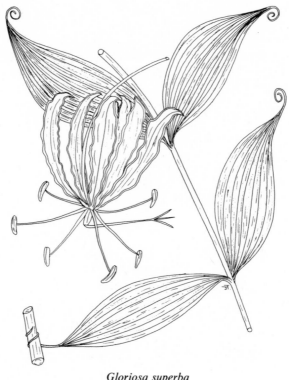

Gloriosa superba

Gloriosa superba L.
Glory lily/Climbing lily
Liliaceae

Description A tuberous root gives rise to a stem (up to 2m) climbing by means of tendril-like extensions of the leaves. The leaves are ovate/long-lanceolate (12 × 2·5cm). The perianth segments of the flowers are linear (up to 7·5cm long) and much crisped. They are at first yellow (subsequently turning red in most forms) and are held horizontally or reflexed back over the stalk. The fruit is a capsule, splitting to reveal the seeds.

Distribution and Habitat Native to tropical Africa and Asia, this plant is commonly cultivated outdoors or in the greenhouse.

Dangers The plant contains alkaloids and ingestion results in gastrointestinal irritation with abdominal pain, nervous excitement and numbness of the mouth. Deaths have occurred.

Related Plants *G. rothschildiana* O'Brien is commonly cultivated and also contains alkaloids. The genus contains some six species.

Narcissus pseudo-narcissus

Narcissus pseudo-narcissus L.
Daffodil
Amaryllidaceae

Description The bulbous underground portion produces several flat, linear leaves (up to 38 × 2cm). The upright stalk bears a single upright/horizontal flower (up to 6cm long); the corona (edge somewhat frilled) and segments are usually different shades of yellow. A large number of cultivated forms exist, some double and with various colour shades. The fruit is a capsule which splits to reveal the seeds.

Distribution and Habitat Native to Europe and commonly cultivated in Europe, Britain and North America.

Dangers Eating the bulbs by mistake for edible bulbs produces severe gastroenteritis with vomiting and purging. Trembling and convulsions may occur.

Related Plants All members of the genus *Narcissus* (about thirty species in all) are considered dangerous. Many other commonly cultivated genera in this family, such as *Galanthus*, *Amaryllis*, *Crinum*, *Nerine* and *Haemanthus* are also said to contain toxic alkaloids.

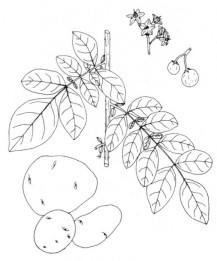

Solanum tuberosum

Solanum tuberosum L.
Potato
Solanaceae

Description The well-known, irregularly ovoid, potato tubers give rise to (or are produced by) a number of somewhat weak, fleshy stems (up to 80cm long) bearing pinnate leaves with up to five ovate/cordate pairs of leaflets. The flowers (white/pale violet) are borne in long stalked clusters. The corolla is wide-spreading (up to 4cm diameter). The fruit, when produced, is a yellowish-green, globular berry (up to 2cm diameter) with up to three cells. In some cultivars the leaves may be somewhat more irregular and dissected.

Distribution and Habitat Various cultivars are commonly grown for food throughout Britain, Europe and North 'America although the plant is originally from South America.

Dangers Any green parts of the plant, especially the skin of greened tubers and sprouts from tubers, contain the toxic alkaloid solanine. These should never be eaten. Even non-green potatoes contain alkaloids but these are at very low levels and mostly lost during peeling. Diseased potatoes may be toxic for other reasons. Gastrointestinal irritation with pain, constipation or diarrhoea and nervous effects such as drowsiness, loss of sensation, weakness, breathing difficulties and paralysis with death may occur.

Related Plants *S. melongena* L. (eggplant) has edible fruit but the plant contains toxic alkaloids. See also entries for *S. carolinense* L. (page 84) and *S. dulcamara* L. (page 81).

Chelidonium majus

Chelidonium majus L.
Celandine poppy/Greater celandine
Papaveraceae

Description The perennial, woody rootstock, clothed in the persistent bases
of previous leaves, gives rise to a branched leafy stem up to about 1m high
which is brittle to the touch, liberating easily the bright orange sap. The
deeply pinnate (five to seven lobed) leaves are crenately toothed and often
rather glaucous on the lower surface. The rather small (2·5cm diameter)
yellow flowers are borne in few-flowered terminal clusters. They have four
petals, two sepals, many stamens and each gives rise to a single capsule (up
to 5cm) containing many black seeds with a white appendage.

Distribution and Habitat Native to Britain, Europe and North Asia but
commonly cultivated both there and in America and naturalised from cultivation. Prefers rich soil, commonly near old houses, on banks, in hedges.

Dangers Although sometimes used as a homeopathic medicine, the sap
causes severe skin irritation and if swallowed causes gastroenteritis. A wide
range of alkaloids, many similar to those found in the *Papaver* poppies
(page 67), have been identified in the sap. It has caused death in humans.

Related Plants The variety *laciniatum* has the leaf lobes deeply and narrowly
cut. Only two species are recognised.

Euphorbia pulcherrima

Euphorbia pulcherrima Willd.
(*Poinsettia pulcherrima* R. Grah)

Poinsettia

Euphorbiaceae

Description Shrub (up to 3m) bearing ovate/lanceolate leaves (up to 15cm) with entire, lobed or toothed margins. The upper leaves are almost entire and coloured bright red when in flower. The tiny flowers are crowded together within a clasping covering, and the discrete masses of flowers are further aggregated into an inflorescence. Bright yellow glands occur on the small (about 8mm) greenish coverings. Flowers are produced in the winter months. Some cultivated forms have white or pink floral bracts.

Distribution and Habitat A commonly cultivated greenhouse and house plant, throughout the temperate zone, frequently used for winter decoration because of its showy red bracts. Native to tropical Mexico and central America.

Dangers Young children have ready access to this house plant. A child (two years old) is reported to have died after eating a leaf. Prior to death the symptoms were vomiting and purgation of the bowels accompanied by delirium. The milky sap is capable of producing blistering of the skin and gastroenteritis.

Related Plants Wild euphorbias are discussed separately on page 96. Other ornamentals such as *E. marginata* (snow-on-the-mountain), *E. cyparissias* (cypress spurge), *E. milli* Ch. des Moulins (crown-of-thorns cactus), *E. lactea* Haw. (candelabra cactus) and *E. tirucalli* L. (pencil, Malabar or spurge tree) also contain irritant juice and are potentially dangerous.

Cannabis sativa

Cannabis sativa L.
Hemp/Marihuana
Cannabinaceae

Description This coarse annual herb (up to 2·5m) has palmately compound leaves with up to seven, dentate, broadly linear leaflets. Male and female plants are separate, the latter having an axillary cluster of small green flowers each ripening into a conspicuous achene. The various cultivars may show very different characteristics.

Distribution and Habitat Commonly cultivated for fibre production, birdseed and oil. Production is usually under licence only, even though the major narcotic-producing strains are different from those for other commercial uses. The plant is widely naturalised in many places in North America and Europe, although originally from Asia.

Dangers The narcotic effect of the resin from hemp is well known. Generally, euphoria, happiness and heightened sensitivity are followed by hallucination, confusion and finally depression and coma. Individuals differ in their reactions. The poison is usually self-administered by smoking dried plant material or resin. Addiction is not usually severe but physical and moral degeneration are frequently found in users of this drug. The greatest resin content is found in the inflorescences of female plants favoured by warm climates.

Related Plants *C. indica* (Indian hemp) is sometimes unofficially considered as a distinct plant, when grown for narcotic production alone.

Chenopodium ambrosioides

Chenopodium ambrosioides L.
Wormseed/Mexican tea
Polygonaceae

Description An annual or perennial much-branched (from the base) herb up to 1m high. Strong-smelling and covered with glandular hairs. The lower leaves are oblong-ovate (up to 9cm long), coarsely dentate with the upper ones sub-entire and tapering into the petiole. The small flowers are massed in spikes (branched on large plants), often with bare stem between the masses of flowers. The fruit is one-seeded and enclosed in the dry, persistent calyx.

Distribution Native to tropical America but now naturalised from cultivation in many places in eastern North America. A form (var. *antihelminticum*) is cultivated for its oil.

Dangers Overdoses of the antihelminthic oil have caused human deaths. The terpene, ascaridol, is the active ingredient in the oil and, when an overdose is taken, causes severe gastroenteritis with pain, vomiting and diarrhoea.

Related Plants The genus contains about 250 species, many being common weeds of cultivation.

64

Fagopyrum sagittatum

Fagopyrum sagittatum Gilib.
(*Fagopyrum esculentum* Moench)

Buckwheat

Polygonaceae

Description An erect, sparsely branched annual up to 60cm bearing simple, broad, sagittate/cordate leaves along the length of the stem. Often appearing almost bushy. The individually tiny white or pinkish flowers are massed into cymose, rather linear, inflorescences. The fruits are up to 6mm long and distinctly three-angled.

Distribution and Habitat Commonly cultivated as a grain or for green manure. Frequently found also in waste places and near habitation. Thought to be native originally to central Asia.

Dangers The flour is used in some places for human consumption, especially in pancake mixes. Although the plant is a well-known producer of photo-sensitivity in animals, most cases of human poisoning appear to arise from an allergic response in certain members of the population. It is possible, however, that a photosensitive component may exist in the reaction. The active substance for photosensitisation may be a napthrodianthrone deriva-tive known as 'fagopyrin'.

Related Plants About eight species are recognised in the genus. The family contains many common weeds.

65

Gelsemium sempervirens

Gelsemium sempervirens (L.) Ait. f.

Carolina jessamine/Yellow jessamine/Evening trumpet flower

Loganiaceae

Description An evergreen, perennial vine (up to about 7m) with lanceolate entire leaves (up to 10cm long). The flowers are fragrant, tubular (up to 4cm long) and yellow, grouped (up to six) in showy clusters. The fruit is a flat capsule (1cm long) opening by two valves from the apex and containing winged, flattened, seeds.

Distribution and Habitat Native to hedgerows and thickets on lower land from Texas to Virginia. A climbing or trailing plant. Sometimes cultivated elsewhere in the open or under glass.

Dangers Nectar sucked from the flowers by children has poisoned them and there is an old record of fatal poisoning supposedly caused by honey from *Gelsemium* nectar. The alkaloids known to be present in the plant are the suspected toxic agents. Death due to respiratory failure follows general symptoms of depression, double vision and dilation of the pupils, and weakness.

Related Plants About three species are described in the genus.

66

Papaver somniferum

Papaver somniferum L.
Opium poppy
Papaveraceae

Description This annual herb has a taproot which produces a simple or branched stem up to 1m tall. The leaves are ovate/oblong with irregular lobing and undulate margins. All are glaucous and the upper ones clasp the stem. The large (up to 18cm diameter) flowers are white or pale lilac, sometimes with a darker basal blotch. The globular or ovoid capsules vary widely in diameter but can be large. The pores occur just under the flattened 'lid' and when they burst allow the many tiny black or white seeds to escape.

Distribution and Habitat Native to some parts of Europe and Asia but introduced widely elsewhere in Europe and America. Only licensed persons may now cultivate the plant but garden forms (subspecies *hortense*, which have the dark blotch on the petals) can still be found in old gardens and derelict sites.

Dangers The drug opium is normally obtained by cutting the unripe capsules and collecting the crude resin which exudes. This contains over twenty different isoquinoline alkaloids such as morphine, codeine and papaverine. Addiction and misuse are frequent and well-known and account for most deaths due to poppies. Alkaloids have been isolated from most species of poppy but these usually differ from those of *P. somniferum* and are present in lower amounts. Potentially all are dangerous.

Related Plants About 100 species are known, many are common weeds and some live in arctic or sub-arctic climates. The common garden 'oriental' poppy is *P. orientale*. *P. nudicaule* (Iceland poppy) and *P. rhoeas* (corn poppy) are also cultivated.

Podophyllum peltatum

Podophyllum peltatum L.
Mayapple/American mandrake
Berberidaceae

Description A fleshy, perennial, rootstock gives rise to one or two large (about 20cm diameter) irregularly lobed, umbrella-shaped leaves. A single white flower, about 5cm across and with six or nine petals is borne between the leaves and gives rise to a fleshy berry (about 4cm long) of a blotchy yellow colour and containing many seeds.

Distribution and Habitat Found in open places throughout the US and southern Canada.

Dangers This plant has frequently been used as a home remedy. The misuse of the resin (extracted from the root with alcohol and precipitated by adding water) called 'podophyllin' will produce drastic gastroenteritis, purging and vomiting. Deaths have occurred. People working daily with the powdered rootstock often develop severe skin reactions with lesions, keratitis (inflammation of the cornea) and conjunctivitis. A large number of toxic ingredients have been isolated, most falling into the chemical groups of the lignans and flavonols. The fruit pulp is used in preserves and is considered edible.

Related Plants The genus contains about four species.

Dangerous Plants Frequently
Growing Wild

The page numbers (given in brackets) refer to the detailed plant descriptions.

Berries and Fruits

Black:

HERB	*Actaea spicata* (71)
	Atropa belladonna (72)
CLIMBER	*Hedera helix* (73)
	Menispermum canadense (74)
SHRUB OR TREE	*Karwinskia humboldtiana* (75)
	Rhamnus catharticus (76)
	Sambucus nigra (77)

Red or pink:

HERB	*Arum maculatum* (78)
CLIMBER	*Bryonia dioica* (79)
	Solanum dulcamara (81)
	Tamus communis (82)
SHRUB OR TREE	*Euonymus europaeus* (83)

Yellow:

Solanum carolinense (84)

White:

Phoradendron flavescens (85)

Seeds

HERB	*Datura stramonium* (86)
CLIMBER	*Momordica charantia* (87)
SHRUB	*Sophora secundiflora* (88)

Leaves or Stem

Aethusa cynapium (89)
Conium maculatum (90)

Underground Parts

Arisaema atrorubens (91)
Cicuta maculata (93)
Oenanthe crocata (94)
Zigadenus gramineus (95)

Contact with Juice

Euphorbia species (96)
Hippomane mancinella (97)
Ranunculus species (99)
Toxicodendron radicans (101)
Toxicodendron vernix (102)

Food Contaminant or Medicinal

Agrostemma githago (103)
Eupatorium rugosum (104)
Haplopappus heterophyllus (105)
Helleborus foetidus (106)
Kalmia latifolia (107)
Lobelia inflata (108)
Mandragora officinarum (109)
Nicotiana trigonophylla (110)
Phytolacca americana (111)
Veratrum viride (112)

Actaea spicata

Actaea spicata L.
Baneberry/Herb christopher/Dolls-eyes
Ranunculaceae

Description A perennial, bad smelling herb with a stout blackish rhizome giving off large, long-stalked, biternate or bipinnate leaves, the secondary leaflets being ovate to three-lobed and with serrated edges. The leaves on the stem are much smaller. When flowering, an erect stem (up to 0·7m) bears terminal (plus occasional lateral) racemes of white open flowers with many long spreading stamens. The berry is at first green, turning blackish and shining, about 1cm long. It contains several flattened, semi-circular, seeds about 4mm wide.

Distribution and Habitat Found in Britain, Europe extending into Norway and parts of temperate Asia, but preferring the colder north-temperate zone. Preferring limestone sites where possible.

Dangers The berries are attractive to children and can cause severe gastro-enteritis with vomiting, diarrhoea and delirium due probably to the toxic essential oil they contain. Death has occurred among children.

Related Plants About eight species are recognised, several being found in North America. *A. rubra* (red baneberry) and *A. alba* (white baneberry) have caused poisonings.

Atropa belladonna

Atropa belladonna L.
Deadly nightshade
Solanaceae

Description A thick perennial root gives rise to a highly branched herbaceous plant up to about 2m high. The large, entire, ovate leaves of the main stems have rapidly developing axillary buds, often giving the misleading appearance that the leaves are in pairs. The dull purple/green tubular, flowers are up to 2·5cm long and borne singly. The ripe fruit is a purple/black berry up to 2cm in diameter.

Distribution Native to Britain and Europe but not widely found even there. The plant is also found in the US as a temporary escape from cultivation. Preferring woods or thickets on calcareous soil or in hedges near old buildings.

Dangers Children have been killed by eating only three of the berries and the whole plant should be considered dangerous due to its alkaloids. These affect particularly the parasympathetic nervous system. Pupils of the eyes are dilated, the heartbeat rapid, the pulse weak, with trembling and excitement. Some hours later or sooner, depending on the amount consumed, prostration, coma and death occur. Alkaloid is present in all parts with the maximum content at maturity. Poisoning by other plants is often wrongly ascribed to *A. belladonna*. The flesh from rabbits and birds which have eaten *Atropa* has caused poisoning on a few occasions.

Related Plants There are only two species in this genus but closely related genera such as *Datura*, *Hyoscyamus* and *Solanum* are also well-known as poisonous.

72

Hedera helix

Hedera helix L.
English ivy
Araliaceae

Description Climbing vine (up to 35m) attaching by adventitious roots to trees, walls and other supports. Leaves are glossy and evergreen. Shrubby forms also occur and plants in flower typically have the adult leaf form. Young leaves are three- or five-lobed; adult leaves are entire. The yellowish-green flowers are borne in umbels from the 'adult' branches and followed by smooth, globular black berries about 8mm in diameter.

Distribution Native to Europe and Britain and grown extensively there and in North America. Many horticultural forms also exist, some recognised as different species.

Dangers The berries are attractive to children and have caused poisoning as also have the leaves, probably due to the presence of the saponic glycoside known as hederagenin. Symptoms are mainly purgative unless larger quantities are consumed when nervous excitement, breathing difficulties and coma may occur.

Related Plants Only about five species of *Hedera* are recognised.

73

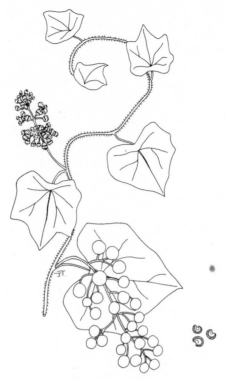

Menispermum canadense

Menispermum canadense L.
Moonseed
Menispermaceae

Description This twining climber (up to 5m) has the general appearance of a grape-vine; but its leaves are entire or have only a few, up to ten, broad lobes rather than the twenty or more blunt teeth of the true grape. The small flowers are greenish-white and massed in axillary panicles up to 4cm across. Although the fruits also bear a superficial resemblance to small purple-black grapes they are distinct in containing only a single, crescent-shaped seed – which gives them their name.

Distribution and Habitat The plant is native to eastern North America where it is found in woods and hedges but fortunately not commonly. Some gardeners may encourage it over fences and gates.

Dangers Children can easily mistake the fruits for grapes, and deaths have been reported in the US.

Related Plants Two species are described in the genus.

Karwinskia humboldtiana

Karwinskia humboldtiana Zucc.

Coyotillo

Rhamnaceae

Description This shrub or small tree (up to about 6m) has elliptical leaves (up to 8cm long) with entire or slightly wavy margins. The small, greenish flowers borne in the leaf axils give rise to dark brownish, ovoid fruits (up to about 1·5cm diameter) containing several seeds, borne in axillary clusters.

Distribution and Habitat This American plant prefers gravelly sites in the southern Texas, California regions.

Dangers Children have been poisoned by the berries which have been known, from Indian times, to produce paralysis. No symptoms may be shown or felt for several days or even weeks after eating. Weakness and leg inco-ordination are followed by paralysis of the motor nervous system. The seeds, and to a lesser extent the fruit pulp, are poisonous.

Related Plants The family contains some other toxic genera.

Rhamnus cathartica

Rhamnus catharticus L.

Common buckthorn/Purging buckthorn

Rhamnaceae

Description A much-branched shrub up to 10m with sharp spines replacing many potential side branches.

The leaves (up to 6cm) are simple, ovate elliptic, with serrate margins.

The female flowers (4mm diameter) have four small petals and grow solitary or in clusters from the leaf axils on the previous year's wood. The berries (up to 1cm diameter) are at first green, turning black when ripe. They contain up to four seeds.

Distribution and Habitat Native to Britain and Europe and introduced into North America as an ornamental, often for hedging. Now naturalised in many places. Frequently growing in woods on chalk, or in scrub and hedges elsewhere.

Dangers The attractive fruits contain a glycoside which yields a strongly laxative anthraquinone on hydrolysis. In excess this effect leads to severe gastroenteritis.

Related Plants *R. frangula* L. (*Frangula alnus* Mill.) (alder buckthorn) is commonly cultivated and *R. purshiana* DC., native in the north-west Pacific coastal region of America, is the source of the laxative 'cascara sagrada'.

76

Sambucus nigra

Sambucus nigra L.
Elder/Elderberry
Caprifoliaceae

Description Shrubby bush/small tree up to 10m. The twigs have prominent lenticels. The pinnate leaves have ovate/lanceolate leaflets up to 9cm long with serrate margins. The conspicuous, (20cm diameter) flat-topped inflorescence consists of small (5mm diameter) creamy flowers followed by globose, black berries (up to 8mm) containing several flattened seeds.

Distribution and Habitat Native to Britain and Europe and common on nitrogen and base-rich soils in waste places, hedges and the edges of woods.

Dangers The roots and stems have produced poisoning in children and the uncooked berries frequently cause nausea although they are often used for wine-making or other purposes and are then considered harmless.

Related Plants Several other species and varieties occur in North America, Britain and Europe, differing in various ways, such as fruit colour and leaf shape. They are also considered somewhat toxic.

Arum maculatum

Arum maculatum L.
Cuckoo-pint/Lords and ladies
Araceae

Description A white, tuberous perennial rootstock gives rise to arrow-head shaped, green (sometimes darker-spotted) leaves (up to 20cm long) borne on long stalks. The flower consists of a green, erect spathe (up to 25cm high) which protects a dark purple or yellowish central spike (spadix).

The actual flowers are protected within the spathe and by the time the red berries (about 5mm diameter) have ripened the spathe has decayed away, leaving only the remnants of its base.

Distribution and Habitat Common in Britain and Europe northwards to Sweden. It grows singly or in small groups under shrubs and in hedges, or along ditches, and is tolerant of deep shade.

Dangers The berries are attractive to children and considered highly dangerous. The active principle is probably in the irritant juice. The symptoms are those of severe gastroenteritis with vomiting, abdominal pain and purging. Weakness, collapse and symptoms of shock have preceded death in some cases. The starch from the roots was formerly used but is somewhat irritant and its use to stiffen clothes was abandoned.

Related Plants About twenty species are known, mostly from the Mediterranean region.

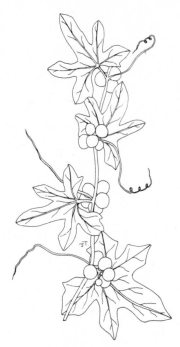

Bryonia dioica

Bryonia dioica Jacq.
White bryony
Cucurbitaceae

Description The large, pale, perennial tuberous rootstock produces stems annually. These are very long and climb by simple tendrils. They bear palmately lobed (five to seven sections) leaves. The small, greenish, female flowers (up to 12mm diameter) are borne in clusters of up to five. They have spreading, triangular sepals, petals some three times longer and bifid stigma. The red berries are up to 8mm diameter and contain several (up to six) large, yellow/black mottled flattened seeds.

Distribution and Habitat Native to Europe and Britain. Found in hedges or shrubby thickets and sometimes locally common on well-drained soils.

Dangers The berries are attractive to children and the roots have been eaten in mistake for parsnips. It has been suggested that only about a dozen berries might be fatal. The symptoms are those of gastroenteritis, with vomiting, abdominal pain and severe diarrhoea, arising from an irritant juice. The active ingredient is probably glycosidic and the substances bryonin and bryonidin have been named.

Related Plants *B. alba* is also mentioned as toxic but the genus contains, in all, some eight species.

Solanum dulcamara

Solanum dulcamara L.
Bittersweet/Woody nightshade
Solanaceae

Description A climbing or trailing slender, woody perennial (up to about 2m) with simple ovate to basally lobed or partly pinnate leaves. The inflorescences are borne opposite the leaves. The flowers are deep purple-blue with yellow-orange stamens and are borne in erect clusters, to be followed by rather translucent, slightly elongated, red, drooping berries up to 1cm long.

Distribution and Habitat Common in waste ground, woods and hedgerows in Britain, Europe and North America.

Dangers The attractive berries have been implicated in the poisoning of children, due to their content of alkaloids. Abdominal pain with constipation or diarrhoea and general gastrointestinal irritation may occur, together with weakness, trembling, drowsiness and paralysis, depending on the amount eaten.

Related Plants The black nightshade (*S. nigrum* L.) and the related *S. americanum* are common weeds (up to 1m tall) with simple dentate or sinuate margined leaves. The flowers are white and followed by green berries ripening to black. These are considered poisonous but the wonderberry or garden huckleberry (*S. intrusum*) is said to be edible although very closely related to *S. nigrum*. *S. pseudocapsicum* L. (Jerusalem cherry) is a common pot-plant, prized for its bright-red berries which are probably toxic and should certainly not be eaten by children. *S. sodomeum* L. (apple of Sodom or popolo) has caused non-fatal poisoning of a child. The berries of *S. triflorum* Nutt (cut-leaf or three-flowered nightshade) and other species with similar sized berries are strictly excluded from canned peas because of their known toxicity. See also entries for *S. carolinense* (page 84) and *S. tuberosum* (page 60).

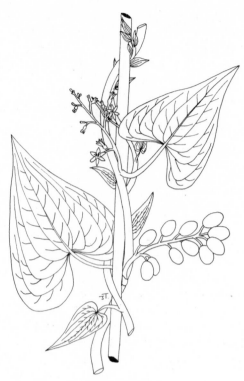

Tamus communis

Tamus communis L.
Black bryony
Dioscoreaceae

Description A large, blackish, fleshy root gives rise to weak, angled un-branched, twining stems (up to 4m). The long-stalked leaves are entire and ovate with a heart-shaped base and a distinct point. There are two 'stipules' at the base. The flowers of the female plant are greenish-yellow and borne in small axillary inflorescences. They are followed by pale-red ovoid berries (up to 12mm) containing up to six wrinkled seeds.

Distribution and Habitat Native to Britain and Europe, common in some places. Usually found twining in hedges, scrub or margins of woods, especially on moist but well-drained fertile soils.

Dangers Children are attracted to the distinctive berries. Symptoms include burning sensations in the mouth and blistering, together with abdominal pain and purging. Deaths have been reported.

Related Plants Only two species are described in this genus.

Euonymus europaeus

Euonymus europaeus L.
Spindle tree
Celastraceae

Description Shrubby trees (up to 6m) with ovate/lanceolate or elliptic leaves (up to 13cm long) with serrated margins. The twigs are green and distinctly four-angled. The small (1cm) greenish flowers are borne in groups of up to ten in axillary cymes. The dark pink, four-lobed fruit is up to 15mm across, opening to reveal an orange aril, containing the seeds (one per lobe).

Distribution and Habitat Common in Britain and Europe to West Asia and south to the Mediterranean regions. Prefers scrubby or woody areas but is present in hedges, usually on calcareous soil.

Dangers The fruits are conspicuous and if eaten produce vomiting, diarrhoea, mental confusion and unconsciousness. This may take several hours to commence.

Related Plants About 120 species of *Euonymus* are known. *E. atropurpureus* Jacq. (burning bush, wakoo) and the evergreen *E. japonicus* Thunb. are commonly cultivated, the latter originally coming from Japan.

Solanum carolinense

Solanum carolinense L.
Horse nettle/Bull nettle
Solanaceae

Description The stems and leaf veins of this branching perennial (up to 1m) bear yellow spines. The simple leaves are ovate but lobed or sinuate at their margins (up to 12cm long). The plant bears stellate hairs. The flowers (2cm diameter) are white or pale-violet borne in a small inflorescence which elongates at maturity. They are followed by yellow berries (up to 1·5cm diameter).

Distribution and Habitat Common in waste and cultivated areas in the southern US and extending into Canada.

Dangers The death of a child from eating the berries has been reported. The plant contains solanine-type glycoalkaloids. The unhydrolysed forms mainly cause gastrointestinal irritation but the alkaloids proper produce nervous effects such as drowsiness, loss of sensation, breathing difficulties, weakness, paralysis and unconsciousness. Intestinal irritation may be severe, with inflammation of the mouth and digestive system, vomiting, abdominal pain and constipation or diarrhoea.

Related Plants Most of the species of *Solanum* (over 1,500 are described) are considered toxic due to the alkaloids which they contain, although some parts may be edible. See also entries for *S. tuberosum* (page 60) and *S. dulcamara* L. (page 81).

84

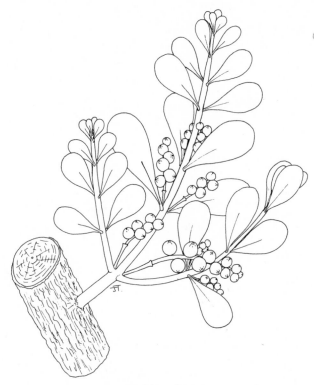

Phoradendron flavescens

Phoradendron flavescens (Pursh) Nutt.
Mistletoe
Loranthaceae

Description A parasitic plant found on a variety of deciduous trees. It forms a rather dense, bushy, outgrowth (up to 40cm across) from the trunks and bears leathery obovate/oblong leaves (up to 6cm) in opposite pairs. The small flowers are borne in short (2 to 5cm) inflorescences in the leaf axils. The fruit is a whitish, almost globular, berry.

Distribution and Habitat Native to North America and commonly also encouraged for its commercial value as a Christmas decoration.

Dangers The berries have caused poisoning when eaten and are attractive and available to children. The poisonous principles are tyramine and beta-phenylethylamine. The symptoms are those of gastroenteritis, leading in fatal cases to failure of the cardiovascular system.

Related Plants Several other species of *Phoradendron* occur in North America. These and the European mistletoe (*Viscum album*) are also considered toxic.

Datura stramonium

Datura stramonium L.
Thornapple/Jimson weed
Solanaceae

Description This coarse herb grows up to 1m high. The large (up to 20cm) ovate leaves have irregular coarse teeth or dentate margins. The flowers (up to 10cm long) are tubular with five pointed lobes and are white or purple (in the variety *tatula*). They are erect and borne singly. The fruit is a spiny erect capsule (up to 5cm long) usually covered with long sharp spines and opening by four slits. It contains many dark-coloured seeds. The variety *inermis* lacks the spines.

Distribution and Habitat Common weed of cultivated places, especially on rich soils in the US and Canada. Less common in Britain but extending in Europe through most of temperate and sub-tropical regions.

Dangers A number of different alkaloids are present including atropine, hyoscine (scopolamine) and hyoscyamine. People are often poisoned by parts or extracts (often used for asthma treatments) from this plant. A small amount (about 5g) of leaf or seed can be fatal to a child. Raw plant material takes longer to act – up to several hours. Thirst and vision disturbance, flushing and nervous twitching, delirium, plucking motion with the hands and a rapid, weak heartbeat are typical symptoms. These may be followed by convulsions, coma and death. In non-fatal cases some symptoms may continue for several days. Children are attracted to the capsules and seeds.

Related Plants About twenty species are known, mostly from central America. *D. metel* has larger flowers and nodding capsule *D. metaloides* is finely hairy and has flowers up to 22cm long. *D. suaveolens* is a shrub up to 5m tall, cultivated as an ornamental.

86

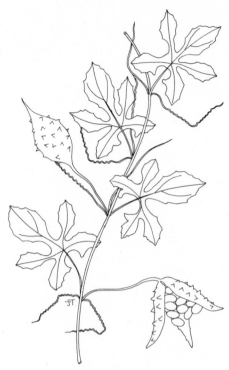

Momordica charantia

Momordica charantia L.
Bitter gourd/Balsam-pear
Cucurbitaceae

Description Climbing or scrambling annual vines with palmately lobed leaves up to 15cm across. The yellow, tubular flowers are unisexual and the female ones are followed by pointed, ovoid warty fruits (up to 13cm long), green at first, ripening to yellow-orange. The pulp is red and contains many thick, compressed seeds (up to 1cm long) which are light grey-brown with prominent patterning.

Distribution and Habitat Naturalised in waste places on sandy soils in the south-eastern, coastal, US; but originally an Old World tropical plant.

Dangers The outer fruit-coat and seeds, but not the fruit pulp, are cathartic, producing gastroenteritis with vomiting and diarrhoea, the symptoms persisting for long periods. In some countries the fruit pulp is eaten.

Related Plants The similar *M. balsamina* L. also has cathartic properties. The genus contains about forty species.

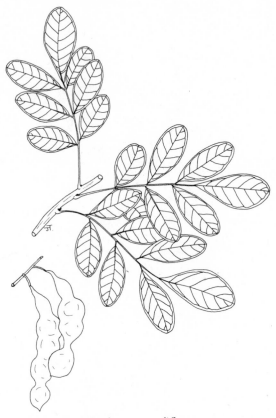

Sophora secundiflora

Sophora secundiflora (Ort.) Lag.
Mescalbean
Leguminosae

Description Evergreen shrub (up to 3m, rarely higher) bearing pinnate leaves with seven to thirteen entire, oblong, leathery leaflets. The strongly scented purple flowers are borne in terminal racemes (up to 10cm long) and followed by a large (up to 18cm long) hard, woody, segmented pod containing hard, bright-red seeds (up to 1·5cm).

Distribution and Habitat Native to hills, ranges and canyons on limestone soil in the southern US.

Dangers The seeds have been used to produce excitement, delirium and prolonged sleep lasting several days. Children are said to have been fatally poisoned by chewing one seed, due to the alkaloids present in the plant.

Related Plants Several other species of *Sophora* are also considered toxic.

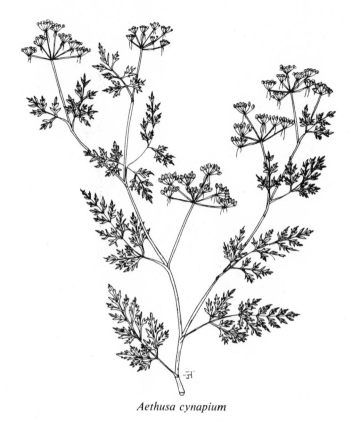

Aethusa cynapium

Aethusa cynapium L.
Fool's parsley
Umbelliferae

Description An annual, branched herb up to 120cm. The finely lined hollow stems bear pinnatifid leaves with ovate segments and an overall triangular outline. The umbels of white flowers are up to 6cm in diameter. The small (2mm diameter) flowers have unequal petals and are followed by a broadly ovoid fruit having broadly ridged and flattened carpels.

Distribution and Habitat Native to Europe and the UK and introduced and naturalised in north-eastern US and south-eastern Canada. Prefers gardens and waste places and is often a weed of cultivation.

Dangers The leaves mistaken for parsley and the roots for young turnips or radishes have poisoned humans, probably due to alkaloids which may be present. The symptoms include incoordination of the limbs and somewhat resemble those of *Conium*. Some workers suggest that it contains coniine.

Related Plants Only one European species exists in this genus.

Conium maculatum

Conium maculatum L.
Hemlock
Umbelliferae

Description The stout stems (up to 3m tall) are ridged, hollow and usually bear purple spots. The large leaves are compoundly pinnate (four or five times). The biggest form a basal rosette and appear very dissected into small leaflets. The small, white flowers of the umbel are followed by laterally compressed fruits with five prominent, wavy, ridges. The root is fleshy, white and normally unbranched. Although often growing as a biennial it can be perennial under favourable climatic conditions. The plant is described as having a 'mousy' odour.

Distribution and Habitat Native to Europe and Britain and introduced and naturalised throughout the US and southern Canada. It grows mainly in damp places, open woods, roadsides and waste areas.

Dangers All parts of the plant are poisonous, due to the presence of various alkaloids. Its roots, stems, leaves and seeds have been mistaken for various edible umbellifers, with fatal consequences. The symptoms are nervous at first with trembling and difficulty in walking, dilated pupils, slow and weak heartbeat; coma and respiratory failure lead to death. Vomiting and convulsions may occur.

Related Plants Only two species are recognised in this genus but the family contains several other poisonous or harmful genera such as *Cicuta*, *Heracleum* and *Oenanthe*.

90

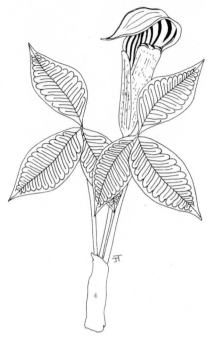

Arisaema atrorubens

Arisaema atrorubens Blume
(*Arisaema triphyllum* Auth. not Torr.)
Jack-in-the-pulpit/Indian turnip
Araceae

Description The large corms (up to 5cm across) produce up to three leaves (some 60cm or more long) with whorled leaflets having cuneate lower sides. The flower (inflorescence) is in the form of a hood-like spathe, which is uniformly greenish-purple inside with pale vertical stripes. The tubular lower extension of this (which may be internally striped with white) surrounds a spadix holding the tiny unisexual flowers. The fruiting head is up to 6cm long and consists of red berries containing one or several seeds.

Distribution and Habitat Native to north-eastern and central US and southern Canada.

Dangers The plant contains fine crystals of calcium oxalate and when parts (for instance the rhizome) are bitten, these are said to enter the mucous membrane of the mouth. The symptoms are intense burning and irritation which normally stops further ingestion so that fatalities do not occur.

Related Plants Other members of the genus *Arisaema* (about sixty species in all) and of other genera in the family Araceae such as *Symphocarpus foetidus* (L.) Nutt. (skunk cabbage) and *Calla palustris* L. (wild calla) have similar properties.

Cicuta maculata

Cicuta maculata L.
Water hemlock
Umbelliferae

Description A bundle of fleshy, swollen, roots gives rise at first to large (up to 1m) leaves formed in a basal cluster and pinnately compound (two or three times) with lanceolate, serrate margined leaflets 5 to 12·5cm long. The erect stem (up to 3m high) only forms when flowering occurs and is hollow except for the plates across the node joints. The swollen base of the stem is characterised by being hollow with thin membranes across it forming air chambers. When cut the stem exudes a toxic yellow oil which smells of parsnip. The umbel inflorescence consists of tiny greenish-white flowers. The fruits are broadly ovoid with the carpels bearing fine flattened ridges.

Distribution and Habitat Found only in wet marshy areas and along streams. This species occurs in the eastern US and Canada.

Dangers The roots have often been mistaken for edible roots, especially by children. The cicutoxin (chemically an unsaturated higher alcohol) acts directly on the nervous system, rapidly (usually within thirty minutes) to produce salivation followed by violent convulsions which distort the body and cause grinding or clamping of the teeth. There is dilation of the pupils and delirium. Abdominal pain and vomiting commonly occur. Death occurs due to paralysis and respiratory failure. Considered very dangerous.

Related Plants All species of *Cicuta* (about six are recognised) are considered highly poisonous. *C. virosa* (cowbane) is a local UK and north and central European species very similar to *C. maculata* L. Several other North American species occur in different parts of the Continent.

Oenanthe crocata

Oenanthe crocata L.
Water dropwort
Umbelliferae

Description A clump of yellowish-white, finger-like tubers (up to 3cm diameter) gives rise to a stout, branched, ridged, hollow, stem up to about 1·5m high. The compound leaves are much divided (up to four pinnate) and may be over 30cm long. The tiny white flowers are borne in compound umbels at the ends of the stems, each individual mass of flowers being almost globular (up to 10cm diameter). The juice of the plant turns yellow when exposed to the air. The seeds are cylindrical, up to 6cm long.

Distribution and Habitat Found in Britain and Europe. Grows in wet places, marshes, ditches and slow streams. Not usually found near chalk or limestone.

Dangers The plant contains the highly toxic oenanthetoxin. Fatalities have resulted from confusion of the plant with celery or the roots with parsnip. Death usually occurs rapidly after a period of convulsions, the pupils may be dilated and salivation occurs. The tubers are sweet-tasted.

Related Plants Other species of *Oenanthe* are considered poisonous, but are probably less seriously so than this particular species. In all, about thirty-five species are described.

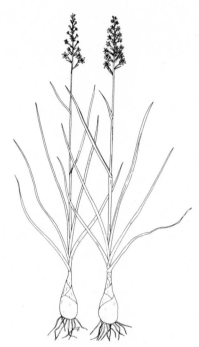

Zigadenus gramineus

Zigadenus gramineus Rydb.
Death camas
Liliaceae

Description A bulb gives rise to several linear, V-creased leaves. The flowers are yellow/white and borne in a raceme at the top of the stem (up to 40cm tall). The perianth is six-membered with spreading lobes which remain attached to the developing fruit. The capsule is three-celled, splitting open to the base at maturity to reveal the numerous small seeds.

Distribution and Habitat Native to open plains and hills in central and southern US.

Dangers Human poisoning is largely a thing of the past and was due to mistaking the plant for edible bulbous plants although all parts are dangerous. Symptoms are those of gastrointestinal irritation with pain, vomiting and diarrhoea followed by muscular weakness, twitching, collapse, breathing difficulties, coma and sometimes death.

Related Plants Considerable confusion exists in the identification of the various species of *Zigadenus* and although some are thought to be harmless they are best all regarded as potentially dangerous.

Euphorbia helioscopia

Euphorbia species
Spurges
Euphorbiaceae

Description Most wild Euphorbias are herbaceous but a few species are woody bushes. All possess an irritant milky sap. The herbs may be annual or perennial and have opposite or alternate leaves of simple, entire or dentate form. The complex, easily recognised, 'flowers' are really inflorescences with the bracts obvious and green to yellow in colour. The individual flowers are very small, a single female flower being surrounded by several male ones each of which consists of only one stamen. The fruit is a three-valved capsule, each valve containing one seed.

Distribution and Habitat Various species are widely distributed, some in temperate and others in tropical regions of both Europe and America. Some species prefer shady woods. Others such as *E. helioscopia* L. (sun spurge) and *E. peplus* L. (petty spurge) prefer open sunny situations in cultivated and waste ground. *E. lathyris* was formerly cultivated for its fruits and is often only doubtfully native.

Dangers The juice causes lesions of the mouth and digestive system producing severe gastroenteritis with purgation. *E. helioscopia* and *E. peplus* have both caused human deaths. The fruits of *E. lathyris* have been mistaken for the true caper and been eaten by children, and have even been pickled and eaten producing severe digestive symptoms. All Euphorbias should be considered potentially dangerous.

Related Plants About 1,600 species are recognised. Cultivated species are mentioned separately under *E. pulcherrima* (page 62).

96

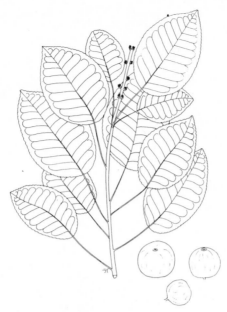

Hippomane mancinella

Hippomane mancinella L.
Manchineel tree
Euphorbiaceae

Description This is a small tree with a rounded crown from which the branches tend to droop. The maximum height is normally about 6m. On older trees the grey-brown bark forms thick scales. The simple ovate leaves (up to 10cm long) have a finely serrated edge. The greenish-yellow (occasionally red-flecked) fruit contains one rather irregular-shaped stone, is up to 4cm in diameter and approaches spherical.

Distribution and Habitat The plant is now almost restricted to the Everglades area of the US having been cut down or destroyed wherever settlers moved into an area.

Dangers The milky sap is highly irritant to skin and eyes, with temporary blindness being common. Reddening of the skin is followed by blistering (often very extensive) in a matter of hours, although sensitivity differs somewhat between people. The fruit does not contain the acrid sap but after consumption it causes abdominal pain, vomiting and bleeding of the digestive tract. Deaths have occurred. The toxic substances are not fully known and it is unlikely that the alkaloid detected in the fruit is the only active substance present.

Related Plants Many other plants in the family are toxic or skin irritant. See entry for *Euphorbia* (page 96).

97

Ranunculus sceleratus

Ranunculus species
Buttercups/Crowfoots
Ranunculaceae

Description These are generally low-growing annual or perennial herbs with alternate, entire or palmately lobed or dissected leaves. The flowers are usually yellow or white, often with five segments to the flowering parts, but the petals particularly may be variable on one plant and between species. The flowers are borne singly and terminal on the stems or in clusters. The many carpels found in each flower ripen to give a cluster of small achenes. Some species creep over the ground, others are solitary or may have tuberous swellings at the base of the stem.

Distribution and Habitat Found in virtually every non-tropical country in the northern hemisphere. Some species prefer the drier areas but many are characteristic of wetter meadows or are completely aquatic.

Dangers The juice of most species is highly vesicant (blister forming) due to the presence of the glycoside ranunculin, which yields the irritant oil proto-anemonin by enzymic action when the plant is damaged. The content varies during growth – often being highest during flowering – and between species. Apart from skin damage upon contact the plant gives severe gastrointestinal irritation if eaten. Mouth and lips will be inflamed. Children have eaten the bulbous parts of some species in mistake for other edible bulbs.

Related Plants About 300 species of buttercup are known, many extremely common in the wild and as weeds in cultivated land, crops and gardens. Probably due to their acrid taste most are left alone by animals and may be conspicuous in fields.

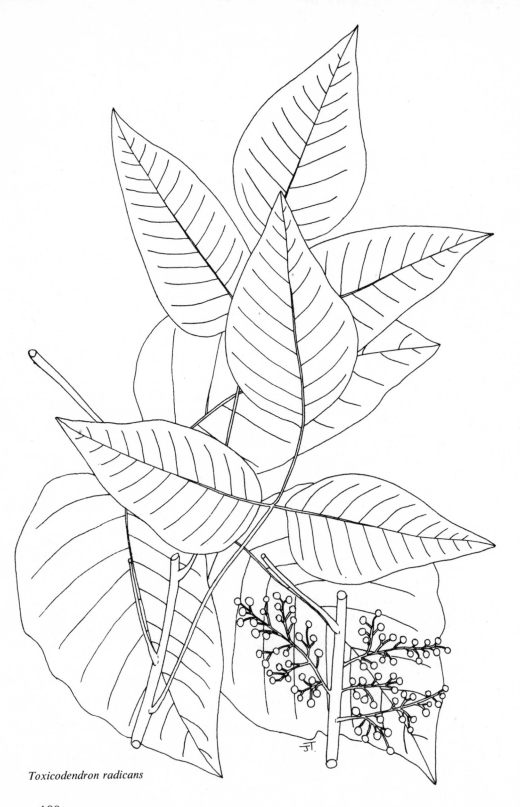

Toxicodendron radicans

100

Toxicodendron radicans (L.) Kuntze
(*Rhus toxicodendron* L.)
Poison ivy/Poison vine
Anacardiaceae

Description Very variable woody shrub or vine with trifoliate leaves. In eastern US a vine or shrub. Var. *littorale* (Mearns) Barkl. is the East Coast form with entire leaflets; var. *radicans* from central US has toothed edges; var. *verrucosum* (Sheele) Barkl. has a pair of deep lobes on the terminal leaflet and is found in Oklahoma and Texas; var. *exinium* (Greene) Barkl. from the Rio Grande has rounded lobes on the leaflets. The small (5mm) whitish green flowers are in multiple inflorescences, male and female on separate plants. The brownish-yellow fruits have a scaly outer coat and a hard white, waxy flesh with black stripes.

Distribution and Habitat Common in the US, mostly on sand dunes, shore edges and low-lying land, east of the Great Basin, Cascade Mountains and the Mojave Desert.

Dangers Damaged plant parts or the juice from them causes dermatitis. The smoke from burning leaves carries droplets of poison and all parts of the plant are toxic at all times. The milky sap is produced in 'resin' canals. Although the four poisons oxidise and polymerise in air the products are still toxic. The dangers follow the typical allergy pattern: usually few symptoms on first contact but rapidly increasing symptoms of itchy red skin and blistering upon frequent contact. Dangerous secondary infections may set in. Eating leaves does not produce immunity to skin contact and leads to severe irritation of the digestive system and even death. People vary considerably in sensitivity to this plant.

Related Plants *T. diversilobum* (T. & G.) Greene is the western poison oak causing similar dermatitis and may interbreed where it overlaps with *T. radicans* (L.) Kuntze. *T. quercifolium* (Michx.) Greene is the equally irritant eastern poison oak.

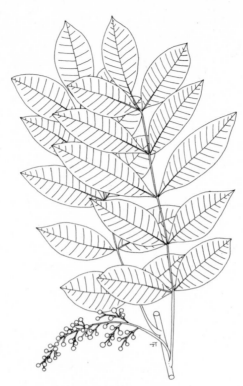

Toxicodendron vernix

Toxicodendron vernix (L.) Kuntze
(*Rhus vernix* L.)
Poison sumac
Anacardiaceae

Description A rather lank shrub (up to about 5m). The compound leaves have seven to eleven leaflets which are bright green and entire margined, contrasting with a bright-red rachis. The small greenish flowers produce glossy, creamy-yellow fruit which hang down from the inflorescence stalks. The waxy mesocarp normally has obvious lines on it.

Distribution and Habitat Found in swamps, bogs and wet ground from southern Quebec to Florida, not extending westward much beyond the Mississippi.

Dangers As for *T. radicans* (page 101) but less likely to be touched due to its habitat.

Related Plants The commonly cultivated (in Europe and North America) species of *Rhus* have toothed margins to their leaves and their red fruits are held erect over the stem apices. They are reputedly non-toxic but some people are somewhat sensitive to their juice.

Agrostemma githago

Agrostemma githago
Corn cockle
Caryophyllaceae

Description An annual plant up to 1m tall with a hairy stem bearing long (up to 12·5cm) narrow hairy leaves. There is a stout tap root.

The large (up to 5cm diameter) reddish flowers are borne singly at the ends of the stems. The calyx tube is stiff and woolly with ten ribs and long (up to 5cm) spreading teeth. The ovoid capsule opens by five teeth to reveal the black, warted seeds (up to 3·5mm).

Distribution and Habitat A weed of cultivation formerly common in wheat fields prior to the use of selective herbicides and seed cleaning. Probably native to southern Europe but now found in Britain and North America as a naturalised weed.

Dangers The seeds contain a saponic glycoside, githagin. Symptoms are those of gastroenteritis with vomiting, diarrhoea and headache. Large amounts produce convulsions, hemolysis (breaking down of red blood cells) and respiratory failure leading to death. Usually only occurs because the seeds are a contaminant in cereals used in food preparation.

Related Plants Of the two species in this genus only *A. githago* L. is widely distributed.

103

Eupatorium rugosum

Eupatorium rugosum Houtt.
(*Eupatorium ageratoides*)
Snakeroot/Rich weed
Compositae

Description An erect, perennial, herb with stiff stems (up to 1·5m tall) arising from a fibrous mass of roots. The simple cordate/ovate leaves (up to 15cm long) have serrated margins and an acute tip. The small white, flowers are borne in composite heads of up to thirty and the heads are grouped in distinctive loose terminal corymbs.

Distribution and Habitat Native to eastern US and Canada, usually in open woods on moist land, usually with a rich basic soil. Spreading particularly after tree felling but not persisting on fully cultivated soils.

Dangers The gradual onset of symptoms such as nausea, abdominal pain, weakness, vomiting, constipation, thirst, and collapse often leading to coma and death, result usually from drinking milk from cows which have eaten the plant. The breath smells of acetone. This is due to forms of the substance known as trematol, a complex unstable substance. The animals also show symptoms of poisoning. The name of the toxin is derived from the tremors accompanying poisoning. The former widespread, but highly local, occurrence of severe poisoning is now reduced by proper control of animals and milk products but could occur under 'subsistence' farming conditions.

Related Plants Over thirty white-flowered species of *Eupatorium* are recognised and identified with difficulty from one another, but only *E. rugosum* and its varieties are thought to be toxic.

104

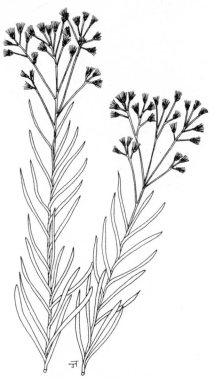

Haplopappus heterophyllus

Haplopappus heterophyllus (Gray) Blake
Rayless goldenrod/Jimmy weed
Compositae

Description A bushy perennial (up to 1·5m) with several stems bearing sticky, simple, linear leaves.

The yellow, composite, heads are borne in small clusters at the stem tips. Each group consists of up to fifteen flowers.

Distribution and Habitat Common on dry range in the southern US and around drainage areas and canals.

Dangers The active ingredient trematol can pass into cow's milk and produce symptoms in humans These consist of a gradual onset of abdominal pain, vomiting and constipation followed by weakness and collapse Trembling, coma and death may occur with the characteristic sweet (acetone) smell to the breath. Proper attention to animals' health and the agricultural marketing system now prevents most outbreaks in humans, although the self-sufficient small farmer may be at risk.

Related Plants *H. fruticosus* is known to contain trematol as also may other species in the genus.

Helleborus foetidus

Helleborus foetidus L.
Stinking hellebore/Bear's foot
Ranunculaceae

Description A stout blackish erect stock produces branching stems up to 80cm high, bearing glands on the upper portions. The plant smells unpleasant. The lower evergreen leaves are almost palmate, with rounded lobes and long petioles with sheathing bases. These shade gradually into entire, ovate and vestigial leaves. The greenish flowers have a globular or bell-shaped perianth, sometimes tinged with red, and several dozen stamens. There are usually about three carpels, which are followed by wrinkled follicles having a distinct beak and containing black seeds bearing a white ridge.

Distribution and Habitat Native to Europe and Britain but also occurring as an escape from gardens and naturalised. It prefers woody or scrub areas on shallow, calcareous soils and is not widely distributed.

Dangers The plant was formerly used as a purgative and antihelminthic medicine but is highly dangerous. The symptoms are those of gastrointestinal irritation with severe purging sometimes leading to weakness, delirium, convulsions and even death, probably due to the cardiac glycosides said to be present in the plant. The names helleborein and helleborin have been given to them.

Related Plants *H. niger* L. (Christmas rose) and *H. viridis* are commonly cultivated and both considered highly poisonous. The genus contains about twenty species, all chalk-loving and considered toxic.

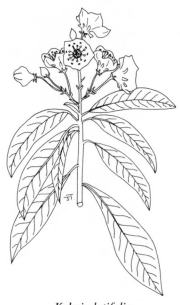

Kalmia latifolia

Kalmia latifolia L.
Mountain laurel/Calico bush
Ericaceae

Description A densely growing shrub or tree (up to 3m) with entire, elliptical, evergreen leaves up to 13cm long. The flowers (about 2cm across) are attractive in white marked with red/purple to complete rose colours, borne in a massed corymbose inflorescence. The flower parts are in fives, with the petals fused into a broad bell-shape. The fruit is a capsule with five cavities, containing a large number of seeds.

Distribution and Habitat Native to the eastern US in mountainous woody areas or cleared patches.

Dangers An extract of a handful of leaves produced toxic symptoms. The active component is probably resinoid. The term andromedotoxin has been used. Others suggest that a glycoside of hydroquinone (arbutin) may cause most of the toxicity symptoms of gastroenteritis, vomiting, abdominal pain, weakness and breathing difficulties. Coma usually precedes death.

Related Plants American Indians used species of laurel for suicide and all species of *Kalmia, Ledum, Leucothoe, Menziesia, Pieris, Rhododendron, Lyonia, Andromeda*, should be considered potentially toxic. Honey from Ericacean pollen is suspected of causing some human poisonings. Plants in many of these genera are commonly cultivated.

Lobelia inflata

Lobelia inflata L.
Lobelia/Indian tobacco
Campanulaceae

Description A much-branched hairy annual (up to 1m) with simple, toothed, broadly lanceolate/oval leaves, the bases of which run down the stem. The small (8mm) blue tubular zygomorphic flowers, are borne in loose terminal racemes and followed by an ovoid (two-celled) inflated capsule, surrounded by the inflated calyx.

Distribution and Habitat A weed of cultivated and waste areas in the eastern US and Canada.

Dangers Many causes of poisoning have arisen from its misuse in folk-medicines. Several alkaloids are present in all parts of the plant. Symptoms include vomiting, pain, feeble but racing pulse, paralysis, transient convulsions, weakness and coma with some deaths. Originally dried and smoked by American Indians.

Related Plants All species of *Lobelia* should be considered dangerous, including those in common cultivation in gardens. Many have large, blue or red, showy flowers.

108

Mandragora officinarum

Mandragora officinarum L.
Mandrake
Solanaceae

Description The perennial, sometimes anthropomorphic, stout taproot produces a rosette of broad, blunt, lanceolate leaves. The flowers arise from the centre of the rosette, each one being bell-shaped, short-stalked and erect. The corolla is up to 4cm long and deeply five-lobed. In the autumn the leaves enlarge (up to 40cm) and become rather more pointed. The fruit is a yellow-orange berry up to 3cm across. There are no separate male and female plants.

Distribution and Habitat Native to south-west and southern Europe and occasionally in cultivation elsewhere. Normally found in waste places, often in stony areas.

Dangers The root and leaves are highly poisonous but the berries are considered edible and even a delicacy. The poisonous substances include hyoscyamine, mandragorin and other alkaloids. Symptoms of poisoning include loss of feeling and insensitivity to pain, heavy sedation leading to coma and even death. Despite the legendary nature of the plant no harm appears to derive from actually digging it up, nor has it been proved to enhance fertility.

Related Plants Two species are sometimes distinguished and the family contains many other poisonous genera.

Nicotiana trigonophylla

Nicotiana trigonophylla Dunal
Wild tobacco/Desert tobacco
Solanaceae

Description A slim, erect herb with sticky, hairy stem up to 1m tall. The ovate leaves (up to 12cm long) at the stem base, either clasp the stem or are sessile. The upper leaves are narrower and smaller. The white or yellowish long-tubed flowers are massed in inflorescence, and open in the day.

Distribution and Habitat Native to dry, desert soils in the southern US.

Dangers The alkaloid present, nicotine, causes mainly nervous symptoms such as twitching, shaking and shivering. Vomiting, diarrhoea, abdominal pain and breathing difficulties are also present. Vision disturbances may occur. Fatality and poisoning have resulted from eating leaves cooked as a vegetable. Chewing leaves or skin-applied preparations from *Nicotiana* species have proved fatal.

Related Plants *N. tabacum* (cultivated smoking-tobacco) is held responsible for many deaths from smoking although these are not probably related to the alkaloids present. All species, including the flowering garden types, probably contain nicotine.

110

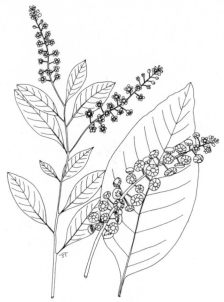

Phytolacca americana

Phytolacca americana L.
(*Phytolacca decandra* L.)
Pokeweed/Pigeon berry
Phytolaccaceae

Description A stout, fleshy, perennial taproot gives rise to a tall (up to 3m) stem, often purple tinged. The entire, ovate, petiolated leaves are pointed at both ends. The long inflorescence raceme bears many small greenish flowers, each with five sepals and ten stamens but no petals. The fruit is a shiny ten-segmented, purple berry, each section containing one seed.

Distribution and Habitat Common near cultivated land on rich soils in the eastern US and southern Canada.

Dangers Some people make pies of the berries but rather inconclusive evidence suggests that they have poisoned children. Other people boil the young shoots as a vegetable, discarding the cooking water, or prepare medicinal extracts from the plant. In susceptible people a burning feeling is produced immediately after eating, followed by vomiting, diarrhoea and gastroenteritis. Sweating, salivation, disturbance of vision, and general respiratory and pulse weakness may, in some cases, precede death. The root is probably the most toxic part and has been mistaken for parsnip or horse-radish. The whole plant is best considered potentially dangerous.

Related Plants About thirty-five species are described in the genus. The strong-growing evergreen *P. dioica*, L. is commonly cultivated in the southern US.

111

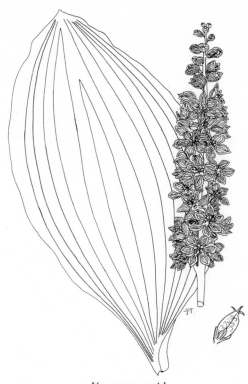

Veratrum veride

Veratrum viride Ait.
White hellebore/False hellebore
Liliaceae

Description A short, thick, perennating, rootstock gives rise to leafy stems (up to 2m tall). The leaves are in three rows, the lowermost oval (up to 30cm long and 15cm wide) and the upper ones more lanceolate. The medium-sized (2·5cm diameter) flowers are greenish and borne in a panicle up to 60cm long. The fruit is a three-celled capsule (up to 2·5cm long) each containing several seeds.

Distribution and Habitat Native to moist pastures and open woods in North America.

Dangers The plant was formerly much used in folk-medicines but often resulted in toxicity. The alkaloids present lower the blood pressure by dilating the arterioles and reducing the heart rate. Symptoms include collapse, salivation, breathing difficulties, burning of throat and mouth, headaches and hallucinations.

Related Plants The European *V. album* L. and other species (up to fourteen are known) are all considered highly toxic.

112

Fungi

The page numbers (given in brackets) refer to the detailed plant descriptions.

Distinct Cap and Stalk Present

Amanita muscaria (114)
Amanita pantherina (115)
Amanita phalloides (116)
Clitocybe illudens (117)
Coprinus atramentarius (118)
Entoloma lividum (119)
Galerina venenata (120)
Inocybe patouillardii (121)
Lepiota morgani (122)
Panaeolus venenosus (123)

Thick Stalk Bearing Irregular Fleshy Mass

Gyromitra esculenta (124)

Spherical Fungus with no Stalk Present

Scleroderma aurantiacum (125)

Amanita muscaria

Amanita muscaria (L.) Fr.
Fly agaric

Description A toadstool with distinct stem and cap (up to 20cm across). The cap is bright yellow to red (rarely white or brownish) with a series of small whitish/yellowish rough scales in a somewhat circular series of concentric rings. Gills white to pale yellow. The white/pale yellow stalk is stout (up to 2·5cm) and long (up to 20cm), arising from a bulbous base above which are a few concentric rings of irregular scales. A ring of membrane near the cap is present in young specimens but may be lost from mature ones. The taste is considered bitter and unattractive.

Distribution and Habitat Common throughout Europe, Britain and North America, usually in woods (often birches or conifers) and occasionally in shrubby areas. Found all through summer but often more abundant in spring or early summer and later, after a dry spell. Single specimens or groups may occur.

Dangers Severe (but rarely fatal) symptoms occur rapidly (up to three hours) usually with abdominal pain, diarrhoea and vomiting. Excessive saliva and perspiration are produced. Breathing may be heavy and the pupils non-responsive to light. Hallucinations and confusion frequently occur and the fungus may be consciously administered for this purpose. Delirium, convulsions, coma and respiratory failure may precede death. Mild cases usually recover in a few hours and even more severe ones may recover after a period of deep sleep, often with amnesia relating to the unpleasant aspects of poisoning. Children may be tempted by this fungus which is commonly represented in their books.

Related Plants See also *A. pantherina* (page 115) and *A. phalloides* (page 116).

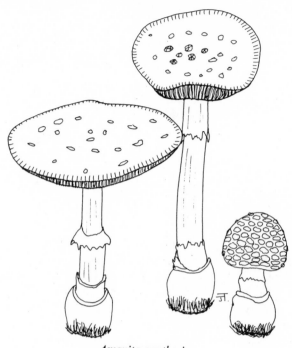

Amanita pantherina

Amanita pantherina (DC.) Fr.
Panther mushroom

Description A toadstool with distinct stem and cap (up to 10cm across). The cap may be somewhat conical at first, becoming flat. It is yellowish, brownish or purplish and covered with regularly spaced whitish scales.

The stem (up to 12·5cm) arises from the bulbous base with some membranous material extending upwards from it. A ring of membranous tissue circles the stem below the cap (it may occur as far as halfway down the stem).

Distribution and Habitat Found in Britain, Europe and North America. Locally common in a few places in the western US, otherwise rare. Preferring conifer woods or open heaths and most likely to be met in spring or autumn.

Dangers This fungus has proved fatal. The symptoms include gastro-intestinal irritation with pain, vomiting and diarrhoea. Perspiration and saliva may be produced and confusion, with hallucinations, is possible. Delirium, coma and death by respiratory failure may occur. The effect is fairly rapid, starting a few hours after ingestion.

Related Plants See also *A. phalloides* (page 116) and *A. muscaria* (page 114). *A. cothurnata* Atk. and *A. pantherinoides* Murr, are considered by some authorities to be identical to *A. pantherina* and are considered toxic.

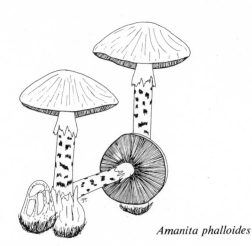

Amanita phalloides (Bull.) Fr.
Death cap/Destroying angel

Amanita phalloides

Description A toadstool with distinct stem and cap (up to 13cm across). The cap is conical at first, sometimes, highly viscid, becoming flat topped or with a slight upturn at the edge. It is smooth (or has a few thin scales) and shades from white through yellowish, greenish, brownish to blackish. The gills are white. The white stalk is up to 20cm long, arising from a bulbous base, the upper margin of which extends as a membrane up the stem. A ring of membranous tissue hangs from the stem just under the cap. There is no strong smell or taste.

Distribution and Habitat Found in Europe and Britain, and it or a closely related species occurs in North America. The rather smaller, white *A. verna* is commonest in most of North America. The toadstools occur in groups or as individuals, normally in open woodland (often beech or oak) usually from June to September.

Dangers As little as a third of a cap can be fatal even when cooked. Symptoms do not develop for many hours (usually about ten but even up to forty hours). There is sudden onset of severe abdominal pain, vomiting and diarrhoea each having blood and mucus in them. Periods of rest occur between the attacks of excessive pain and vomiting. Collapse, with pain occurs and coma and death may follow in up to eight days, preceded by jaundice, cyanosis and low skin temperature. Mortality is very high as the toxins, amanitine and phalloidine, are absorbed prior to the effects being shown. Recovery may take a month and the cell damage may cause changes in body organs which persist much longer.

Related Plants *A. verna* (Bull.) Quel., *A. virosa* (Fr.) Quel., *A. bisporiger* Atk., and some other 'species' closely similar to *A. phalloides* are all considered highly toxic even where they can be 'technically' distinguished from it. Extracts of *A. verniformis* Murr. and *A. virosiformis* Murr. have similar effects to *A. phalloides* (Bull.) Fr. The toxins of *A. brunnescens* differ from those of *A. phalloides*.

116

Clitocybe illudens

Clitocybe illudens (Schw.) Sacc.

Description This toadstool has a stalk and cap. Both cap and stalk are bright yellow/orange and the gills extend slightly down the stalk. When placed in a dark room they can be seen because they are luminescent.

Distribution and Habitat Common in the eastern US and Canada. It grows on old hardwood tree stumps, often in dense groups where the caps overlap one another.

Dangers The symptoms consist of vomiting, starting after a few hours and continuing for several more. Diarrhoea may occur and lead to exhaustion and collapse. It has not been reported as fatal.

Related Plants *C. sudorifica* Pk. and *C. morbifera* Pk. produce similar symptoms plus excessive saliva and perspiration. Occasionally, visual disturbance, abdominal pain and purging may occur. *C. dealbata* and *C. rivulosa* are listed as poisonous, perhaps deadly, and *C. cerussata* is doubtfully poisonous.

117

Coprinus atramentarius

Coprinus atramentarius Fr.
Ink cap

Description A toadstool with stalk and cap. The whitish-brown cap (some 5cm across and 7·5cm tall) is at first closed about the stalk but opening to a bell-shape. Some scales may occur towards the apex and the margin is somewhat grooved. The white gills soon turn black and disintegrate into a fluid. The white stem elongates as the cap matures and may reach 20cm. It has a distinct ring below which the stem is scaly and hollow.

Distribution and Habitat Found commonly in the UK and North America growing in rich soil at the base of trees or in open fields and gardens. Found from mid-summer to late autumn, singly or in groups.

Dangers This toadstool has occasionally caused only cardiovascular upsets but is usually noted for its ability, in certain persons, to produce extensive reddening of the face and body, and speeding pulse rate, if any form of alcohol is consumed while its effects remain in the body (which may be many hours).

Related Plants Records suggest that the normally edible *C. comatus* Fr. (shaggy mane) may, very rarely, produce some intoxication. *C. micaceus* (glistening ink cap) is listed as slightly poisonous.

118

Entoloma lividum

Entoloma lividum (Bull.) Sacc.
Livid entoloma

Description A toadstool with stalk and cap. The cap is a dull yellowish-grey colour, very fleshy and up to 12·5cm across. It is at first rounded but flattens out and has a wavy edge when mature. The gills and spores are pinkish but the flesh is white. The smooth, stout, often curved, white stem (about 7·5cm long) is usually rather thicker towards the base and, when mature, tends to become brittle and hollow.

Distribution and Habitat Found in Britain, Europe and North America. Most likely to be met in grassy places around hardwood trees (beech and oak) during summer and early autumn.

Dangers The symptoms are gastroenteritis, vomiting, pain and diarrhoea, starting soon after being eaten. Weakness and some liver damage may occur, with serious results.

Related Plants *E. sinuatum* (Bull.) Quel. is also considered toxic. This species is difficult to distinguish from *E. lividum*. The genus is best regarded as doubtful.

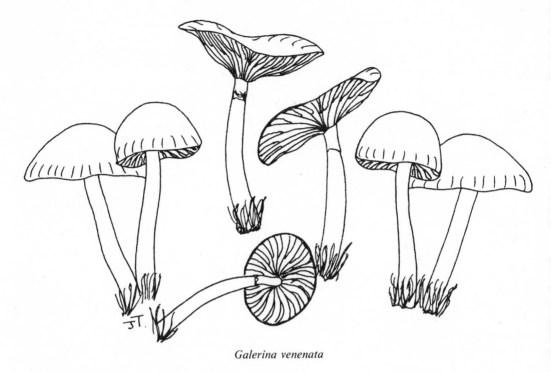

Galerina venenata

Galerina venenata A. H. Smith

Description A toadstool with stalk and cap (up to 3·5cm across). The cap is convex when young, expanding to flat or slightly curved up at the edges. The surface is smooth and moist, light brown fading to yellowish buff. The gills are at first golden yellowish-brown turning a dull light brown. The stalk is up to 4cm long, thin (up to 5mm diameter) and brownish in colour.

Distribution and Habitat Described originally from Oregon, growing in a large group on a lawn, and not fully known elsewhere.

Dangers A large handful produced (starting some ten hours later) extended (up to seven days) vomiting. Greater amounts also caused diarrhoea and progressed to convulsions, jaundice, lung edema and coma. The intestines became paralysed. The patient just survived, with extended hospital treatment. Nearly all the body systems were affected.

Related Plants The genus *Galerina* is separated from the non-poisonous *Conocybe* by the cuticle, which is filamentous in the former and cellular in the latter. All are small, fragile fungi and both genera were formerly included in the genus *Galera*.

120

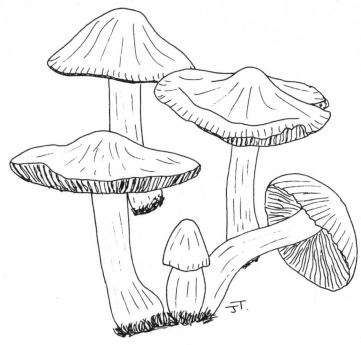

Inocybe patouillardii

Inocybe patouillardii Bres.
Red-staining inocybe

Description A toadstool with stalk and cap (up to 7cm across). The cap develops from conical to flattened with a central hump as it matures. The edge is often folded or wavy. It is at first whitish, becoming yellowish and slowly staining red when damaged or with age. Silky fibrils may occur on the surface. The crowded, narrow, gills are whitish at first, becoming greenish-brown. The smooth stalk is up to 8cm long, swollen at the base and white, but eventually staining red.

Distribution and Habitat Found in Britain and Europe. Prefers woods or grass around trees (especially beech on calcareous soils). Occurs from early summer to autumn.

Dangers Although not normally picked due to its rather small size and lack of any really close resemblance to edible species it has poisoned 'experts' and fatalities are recorded. The symptoms are gastroenteritis, with vomiting and diarrhoea. In severe cases slowing of the heartbeat, respiratory difficulties and coma may occur.

Related Plants Several species are recorded as toxic, including *I. infida* (Pk.) Earle, *I. geophylla*, *I. infelix* Pk. and *I. fastigiata* and the genus is best regarded as poisonous.

121

Lepiota morgani

Lepiota morgani Pk.
(*Lepiota molybdites* (G. Meyer ex Fr.) Sacc.)

Morgan's lepiota

Description This large toadstool has a stalk and cap (up to 25cm across). The cap is at first subglobose expanding to convex and buff-coloured. The surface later becomes scaly. The flesh is white, thick and firm. The gills are white at first, becoming green. The stout stalk is up to 20cm long, with a swollen base, smooth surfaced and white or brown tinged. There is a firm, thick, white ring around the stem, which tends to become loose.

Distribution and Habitat Found in the US and Canada. Usually in grassy places and open woods, sometimes in large groups or rings.

Dangers Even a small bite of this toadstool, raw or cooked, produces abdominal pain, vomiting and diarrhoea. In most people symptoms appear in an hour or so, others seem unaffected by this fungus. Deaths have occurred. Intense thirst and symptoms of shock have also been described.

Related Plants *L. nauciniodes* Pk. is generally considered edible but has possibly produced poisoning. *L. schulzeri* (Kalchb.) Sacc. produces vomiting. The parasol mushroom (*L. procera*) is considered completely edible. *L. cristata* (crested lepiota) and other small species are considered doubtful.

122

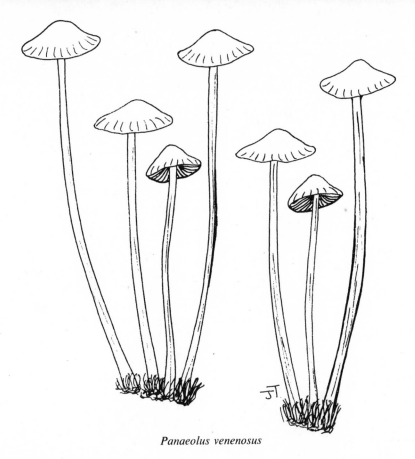

Panaeolus venenosus

Panaeolus venenosus Murr.

Description A small toadstool with stalk and cap. The cap is almost hemi-spherical, smooth, whitish-grey and sometimes tinged with yellow, up to about 3cm across. The gills are rather unevenly black when ripe due to the uneven maturity of the spores. The stalk is thin and hollow, whitish, up to 10cm long, sometimes tinged with golden-yellow or red.

Distribution and Habitat Found in North America, commonly on lawns and as a contaminant in mushroom beds, and on dung.

Dangers Symptoms appear rapidly and consist of muscular incoordination, visual and hallucinatory disturbances and excitation or depression, with loss of control. A subsequent amnesia may occur regarding some of these events. The effects wear off, usually without serious effects.

Related Plants *P. papilionaceous* and *P. subbalteatus* (Berk et Br.) Sacc. are considered identical to *P. venenosus* Murr. *P. semiglobatus, P. papilionaceous* Fr. and *P. camplanatus* (Fr.) Quel. and other species are also considered toxic. Identification of the species is something of a problem and all members of the genus are best regarded as extremely doubtful.

Gyromitra esculenta

Gyromitra esculenta Fr.
(*Helvella esculenta* Fr.)
False morel/Lorchel

Description A very irregularly shaped toadstool with a thick, hollow, coarsely ridged stem bearing an orange-brown fleshy mass (up to about 9cm diameter) with irregular, loose or tight, convolutions on the surface.

Distribution and Habitat Found in Europe, Britain and North America. Often in sandy soil under conifers.

Dangers This fungus shows considerable variation in toxicity and is described as edible in some countries, with some possibility of sensitisation to a second sample. Fatal poisonings have been reported. Symptoms are those of gastrointestinal irritation with vomiting, diarrhoea and weakness, appearing several hours after the fungus is eaten. Severe poisoning causes liver and kidney damage with evidence of damage to the red blood cells.

Related Plants This fungus bears a superficial resemblance to the edible morel (*Morchella esculenta* Fr.). *G. gigas* is also considered poisonous.

124

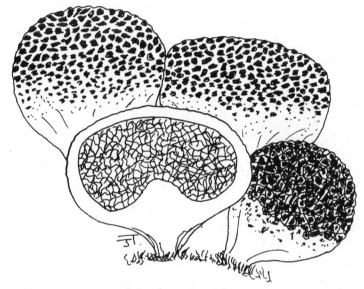

Scleroderma aurantiacum

Scleroderma aurantiacum Pers.
Common earth ball

Description A spherical fungus (up to 15cm diameter but usually not more than 7·5cm). The surface is frequently criss-crossed by cracks or scaly. The outer skin is thick and tough or leathery.

Flesh is white at first then greyish to purple-black and finally brownish.

Distribution and Habitat Common in bushy woods and on heaths, appearing from midsummer to autumn. Found in Britain, Europe and North America.

Dangers Even when cooked this fungus has produced vomiting, abdominal pain, weakness, numbness, sweating and muscular spasms. Vomiting relieved the symptoms and the patient recovered. Some people consider the fungus edible.

Related Plants *S. cepa* Pers. is also toxic.

3 Plant Poisons

A poison can be described as a substance which destroys life or injures health. Such a simple definition can give no indication of the time scale of the effect. In common usage we tend to think of a rapidly acting substance with perhaps only a few minutes, or at the most a few hours, before the effect is shown. Many poisonous substances, however, work only slowly and insidiously, gradually killing off vital cells in the body until finally, perhaps after years of slow progress, the deadly effect is manifest. Most of the familiar poisonous plants contain substances which fall into the category of rapidly acting poisons but it is worth remembering that there are some plants which only produce harmful effects on a much longer time-scale.

The Response to Poison

One problem which arises when discussing the effects of poisonous plants is the variation found in their effects on different people. This arises from two major causes.

Firstly, people differ in their sensitivity to poisons. If a person is in poor health, or has an inefficient liver or kidneys, he is clearly more likely to show symptoms because his body is less able to detoxify or eliminate poisonous substances, or to stand the general shock to the bodily system which they cause. Then, with nearly all poisons there is a relationship between the amount consumed and the severity of the symptoms – the more that is eaten the worse the effect. This is usually also related to the person's size. We would expect a tiny baby to be harmed by small amounts of a poison which might have very little effect on a large adult. Nor should we forget the effects of age. A young body may recover more rapidly or, conversely, carry the damage caused by the poisonous substance for the rest of its life. Which of the two effects occurs depends mostly on the type of damage caused by the poison and very little upon the individual person.

Secondly, even a particular species of plant will differ in the amount of poison it contains. Unlike the doctor's pills, a given weight of plant material does not always contain the same amount of poisonous ingredients. Also, instead of being evenly distributed about the plant these may be concentrated in one or more parts – the fruits, seeds, leaves, stem or roots. The amount may vary during the growing season from low to high levels. This may happen in some regular way during the growth cycle of the plant or, even worse, vary according to the prevailing weather conditions during the season. We often find also that different strains of the same species of plant may have widely different amounts of poisonous substance in them, even when grown under identical conditions.

What criteria can be used, then, when discussing poisonous plants? Firstly, we can consider known and proved cases of death, or severe poisoning, which have been properly documented – albeit often done many years ago and perhaps even under rather odd circumstances such as the classic apple-pip poisoning case, where someone stored up a cupful of apple seeds and ate them in one go, resulting in cyanide poisoning. One or two at a time would not have had this effect. Secondly, we can consider scientific data concerning known toxic substances which occur in plants, even perhaps in the absence of full documentary proof of actual death due to ingestion. Thirdly, we can take the circumstantial evidence, statistical correlations and even informed guesses, based on known botanical relationships between plants. There is no really hard and fast rule, apart from always using common sense and erring on the side of caution – once the spark of life is extinguished it cannot be rekindled, even by modern medicine.

Poisonous Substances in Plants

An enormous literature exists concerning the chemical nature of plant poisons. For convenience they can be grouped together according to certain chemical similarities.

Alkali-like poisons (Alkaloids)

Most people have heard of caustic soda, a cleansing agent which burns the skin and which is an alkali (the exact opposite of an acid). When chemists started studying poisonous plants they found certain substances which, although incapable of burning skin, did have a few of the more obscure chemical properties of the alkalis. So they called such substances 'alkaloids' and this rather poorly descriptive term has been retained, by common usage, over the years. Alkaloids are very complex substances and over the years more than 5,000 different types have been found in plants. Indeed, the most modern biochemical techniques are needed to separate the various alkaloids which may occur even in a single plant. All contain the element nitrogen and nearly all have a strong pharmacological action upon animals. It is suggested that about 10 per cent of all plant species may contain alkaloids, and the same alkaloid may occur in several different related species and even, occasionally, in widely separated genera.

Sugar compounds which affect the heart (Cardiac Glycosides)

The term glycoside is used to describe any substance in which a sugar is attached, by a firm chemical bond, to some other type of molecule. Some of these glycosides have the ability to affect the action of the heart. Over the years some 400 different ones have been isolated from plants, mostly from the lily, foxglove and oleander families. Like some of the alkaloids, many of the well known cardiac glycosides have been given 'common' names (such as digitoxin and oleandrin) – their strict chemical names would be meaningless to all but the specialist biochemist, even where the structure is actually known.

Sugar compounds which liberate cyanide (Cyanogenetic Glycosides)
Another important group of glycosides are those which give off cyanide when acted upon by special enzymes. When intact these substances are usually harmless but many plants (particularly when damaged), micro-organisms and animals produce the necessary enzymes. A wide range of plants possess these glycosides, although the amount present varies from species to species and even from strain to strain of the same species. Weather conditions and how plants are handled can widely affect their cyanide contents.

Toxic proteins in plants (Phytotoxins)
These poisons are unusual in being large protein molecules rather than the much smaller molecules of most toxins. Like other proteins they are denatured by extensive heating and thereby rendered non-toxic. Only a few plants (the castor and precatory beans, for example) produce phytotoxins but those that do are amongst the most poisonous known. The toxic plant proteins, unlike most snake venoms and bacterial toxins of similar nature, are often readily absorbed from the digestive system without undergoing the usual digestive breakdown. This makes them very dangerous when eaten.

Irritant Oils
A glycoside is present in several members of the buttercup family which is itself harmless but which readily undergoes enzymic attack to give an unstable, highly irritant oil, protoanemonin. Glycosides of the cabbage family liberate different substances (mustard oils) containing the isothiocyanate grouping, which are also strongly irritant. Non-glycosidic irritant oils, such as oil of wintergreen and wormseed oil, occur in some plants.

Substances causing enlargement of the thyroid (Goitrogens)
Several plants, in particular members of the genus *Brassica*, contain substances which can inhibit the uptake of iodine into the thyroid gland. This results in a lack of the thyroid hormone and eventually leads to a swelling of the gland as the body tries to maintain its correct level of thyroxine. One of the most potent goitrogenic substances found in the cabbage family is known by the formidable chemical name of L-5-vinyl-2-thiooxazolidone. The chemically simpler 'thiocyanates' can also cause trouble.

Oxalates
Many plants, especially the *Arum* family contain tiny crystals of insoluble calcium oxalate. When these are chewed intense irritation and burning is

produced, as with the dumbcane (*Dieffenbachia*). In other plants the oxalates are more readily soluble and easily enter the blood stream to cause direct or indirect (due to kidney damage) poisoning. Many plants contain small amounts of oxalic acid or its salts which are not sufficient to be harmful. Some of the dangerous ones, however, may contain over 10 per cent.

Resinous substances (Resinoids)
These complex substances have only a few features in common. They do not dissolve in water and when extracted from the plant are semi-solid at room temperatures but readily burned or melted. *Cannabis* resin is typical in properties and in its ability to cause poisoning. Many resinoids are chemically incompletely known.

Glycosides affecting the blood
Another group of glycosides have the sugar linked to a derivative of the substance coumarin. Coumarin itself is the chemical responsible for the characteristic smell of new-mown hay, and I might add, the aroma of certain herbal teas. A typical effect of this type of glycoside is that they are capable of reducing the ability of the blood to clot. They are probably one of the active substances in poisoning by, for example, *Daphne* and *Aesculus*.

Soap-like glycosides (Saponins)
These complex glycosides derive their name from their ability to form a soapy foam when shaken with water. Such substances occur in widely separated genera of plants. Fortunately they are not readily absorbed by an undamaged digestive system but once in the blood they readily cause destruction of the red blood cells.

Amino acid compounds
Most readers will have heard of the normal amino acids, forming the building blocks of the proteins which are so essential to life. Many plants, however, contain related, but slightly unusual amino acids, some of which are highly toxic. Although widely scattered throughout the plant kingdom, they are involved in some cases of severe poisoning, such as that caused by *Amanita* and *Blighia*.

Sensitivity to light (Photosensitisation)
The so-called 'primary' photosensitisation occurs when a plant substance enters the body and this directly causes an animal to become abnormally sensitive to light, producing serious skin damage if the animal is exposed to bright sunlight. The liver-produced (hepatogenous) photosensitisation occurs when a plant substance damages the liver so that normal components of the blood, such as the breakdown products of chlorophyll, continue to circulate in the blood instead of being removed from it. These products cause the sensitivity to light and consequent skin damage. In both cases the symptoms do not develop in the absence of light.

Miscellaneous Poisons

As with all classifications of natural substances there remains a group of odds and ends which may occur only in one or two species of plant but which can, nevertheless, be the cause of serious poisoning. The toxic substance trematol can be passed from plants, via cow's milk, to humans. The coloured compound gossypol can enter cotton seed oil. Unusual compounds of nitrogen occur in sweet peas, and so on. Even in the 1970s many plants are toxic without the active principle being clearly known.

Effects of Plant Poisons

When considering the effects of plant poisons it is important to remember two things. Firstly, the proper functioning of the human body is the result of the integrated activity of a number of distinct systems. A person can die even when only one system is affected by the poison, but between the systems there may be both immediate effects and those developing after hours, days or even months or years. Recognition of rapidly acting substances as poisons is relatively easy. Those with delayed effects are much more difficult to prove.

Secondly, poisons which act mainly on different body systems may produce symptoms of other classes of poisons because of the interacting control systems operating in the normally functioning human body. Many poisonous substances, of course, are toxic to all living cells and the major symptoms they produce depend almost entirely on where in the body they accumulate and act.

Nervous System

This system is concerned with the reception of stimuli (from both outside and within the body) and with controlling the body's responses to such stimuli. Anatomically we distinguish the brain, spinal cord and the 'nerves' themselves but what is more relevant is the physiological distinction into the somatic (voluntary) nervous system and the autonomic (mainly self-controlling) nervous system, with the brain-centres correlating the overall activities of the body.

It is quite possible for the body to maintain life without voluntary control, as in the state known as coma which is technically living but without the higher responses of consciousness. The autonomic system supplies the glands, visceral ('organ') muscles and the cardiac muscles. Many of these have a double system which works antagonistically – the sympathetic which stimulates muscles to contract more strongly or more often, and the parasympathetic which reduces the frequency or strength of the muscle contractions. In theory and in practice, poisons acting on one of these systems can, to some extent, be counteracted by poisons acting on the other.

The control of heartbeat is particularly important. When the SA (sinu-atrial or pacemaker) node is stimulated by its parasympathetic nerve (the vagus) it causes a slower heartbeat by reducing the frequency and strength of the heart muscle contractions. The sympathetic system, acting on both the SA and AV (atrioventricular) nodes, increases heartbeat frequency and strength.

Connections in the brain enable the cerebral cortex (thinking centres) to have some influence upon the autonomic system by way of its overall controlling centre, the hypothalamus. For instance this is the way in which emotions can effect the development of symptoms in allergic states.

Respiratory System

The air-conducting passages passing from the nose and mouth down the trachea to the main bronchi, form a preconditioning system which cleans, warms and moistens the air before it reaches the lungs. The latter are elastic bags with a very large internal surface area due to the presence of the alveolar sacs. Gaseous exchange takes place between the air and the blood in the capillaries (tiny tubes) of the lung's blood circulation, with carbon dioxide passing out from the blood and oxygen passing into it. The lung volume passively follows the contraction of the diaphragm and external intercostal muscles, which increase the chest volume during inspiration and its relaxation during expiration.

Clearly, any reduction in the diameter of the air passages (as occurs during asthma) will result in decreased gaseous exchange and 'shortness' of breath. Normal respiratory movements are controlled by the rhythmical discharge of impulses from the autonomic nervous system. The level of carbon dioxide in the blood is an important controlling factor in the activity of the respiratory centres in the brain. Nerve impulses from the higher centres of the brain and other parts of the body, such as nose and throat, can also affect the respiratory movements. An upset in these, for instance during vomiting under the influence of poisons, can result in the vomit material finding its way into the lungs and blocking the air passages, with serious or fatal results.

Vascular System

This is the distribution system for food materials, respiratory gases, waste products and protective and hormonal chemicals round the body. It is the path that most active poisons follow after absorption from the gut, and the smallest extremities of the system, the capillaries, are involved in the actual interchange of these substances. The flow is maintained by the pumping action of the heart with its double circulation system – the pulmonary one to the lungs and the systemic to all other regions.

The flow of blood in the system affects the heartbeat. Greater return of venous blood accelerates heartbeat while increased arterial pressure causes a slowing of the heart's action and consequent fall in blood pressure. Cardiac output can be altered by changing the rate of heartbeat and the strength of each individual beat. Both blood pressure and volume flowing are strongly influenced by the tone of the walls of the peripheral circulation system and this tone can be altered, for instance in a state of allergy or when certain poisons affect the autonomic nervous system.

Apart from the respiratory gases other blood-borne chemicals, such as the hormone adrenaline, will directly and indirectly affect the heart's action. Plant poisons may have a direct effect too.

The clotting of blood involves a complex series of reactions. Briefly, the substance thrombin is liberated from prothrombin by the action of thromboplastin. Thrombin can then liberate insoluble fibrin threads from fibrinogen, but calcium must also be present. Fibrin forms the framework of the clot and platelets from the blood attach to it. The clot shrinks and adhers at the point of injury. Certain toxic substances in plants can upset clotting and cause hemorrhages. Other toxins from plants can agglutinate (stick together) red blood cells; yet others can break down (hemolyse) the red blood cells.

Liver

The liver produces bile which passes to the gall bladder and is finally discharged, after some changes in its composition, into the intestine where it aids digestion. Food materials from the digestive system enter the liver in its blood supply. In the liver some substances are stored, some are passed on into the general circulation and others, including some toxic susbstances, are subjected to various metabolic changes.

Many toxic plant materials entering the blood from the digestive system pass to the liver and cause damage to it. This may result in other substances, normally detoxified by the liver, being allowed to circulate in the blood, for instance in poisoning by certain plants. Damage to the liver may be rapidly fatal or progressive over a long period of time. Poisonous substances not detoxified by the liver may find their way to the kidneys and damage them, again with serious or fatal consequences.

Kidneys

The kidneys serve as filtration units for the blood. About a quarter of the blood's flow of each cardiac cycle is passed through the kidneys. There, some of the fluid part of the blood, in particular water, salts and other small molecules, pass across the walls into the kidney tubules. The blood vessels form extensive networks around the highly convoluted kidney tubules, enabling the blood to reabsorb essential nutrients back from the liquid in the tubules. Various other syntheses of waste products and their secretion into the tubules take place in the kidneys. Eventually the liquid in the tubules becomes the urine, flowing down the ureters, to be stored in the bladder until lost by micturation. The 'filtered' blood leaves the kidneys by the renal vein.

Digestive System

The various parts of the digestive system are lined by cells with differing functions. In all cases, however, this lining must be intact since only broken-down food material normally passes through the walls into the blood system. In the mouth, mechanical and some chemical (due to enzymes secreted by the salivary glands) breakdown of the food occurs. There is also production of slimy mucin (as there is elsewhere in the system) which lubricates the food to allow its easier passage along the system.

The oesophagus is a muscular, mucous-secreting tube conveying the food into the stomach via the cardiac sphincter. The stomach acts as a reservoir for food and mixes it with the gastric juices, which promote food breakdown. Its wall can absorb some simple substances such as water, alcohol and glucose. These enter the blood vessels supplying the stomach wall.

Vomiting, caused by many plant poisons, as well as by psychological and other influences, is a reflex action. A nerve impulse, from irritated parts of the digestive system, passes to the vomiting centre in the medulla oblongata. This sends out impulses to the vagus nerve, causing the oesophagus, cardiac sphincter and the body of the stomach to relax and the pyloric part of the stomach to contract strongly. The spinal nerves stimulate the abdominal muscles to contract and the phrenic nerve causes descent of the diaphragm to compress the abdominal cavity. The stomach contents are emptied by the subsequent compression forces.

In the small intestine many further enzymes are liberated into the digesting food, and nutrients are absorbed into the blood stream. Contraction of its muscular walls move the food residue along the gut. The absorbed materials in the blood pass to the liver but some substances enter instead the lymphatic system, and follow a different path.

In the large intestine water and salts are reabsorbed to conserve the body's fluids and dry the faeces. Upsets to the speed at which the food material passes along the digestive tract, to the extent of its digestion and to the amount of water extracted from it, are contributory aspects in constipation and diarrhoea – both common symptoms of plant poisoning.

The gut system, in particular the intestines, contain many sorts of micro-organisms, some of which seem definitely beneficial to health. The wrong microbes, and occasionally the activities of normal microbes, acting on substances in the food, can result in digestive upsets and symptoms of poisoning. Many plant poisons actually need to be chemically changed by enzymes before they become fully toxic. The source of these enzymes may be the food, the microbes in the gut or the body itself.

Muscles

All actions involving any type of movement in the body are the result of the contraction or relaxation of muscles. The voluntary muscles bring about purposeful movements, under the control of the higher centres of the brain. Impulses flow along the autonomic nervous system supplying the muscles in the organs and parts of the body which are not directly under voluntary control, but which are essential to its proper functioning and integrated activities. Toxic substances acting upon the nervous system can therefore bring about a wide variety of effects by their influences upon the extent, speed and co-ordination of muscle contractions.

Treatment of Plant Poisoning

Before starting treatment for poisoning it is, of course, necessary to be reasonably sure that poisoning has actually occurred and for this a knowledge of the events prior to the development of the symptoms is almost essential. With children their mothers or friends usually know what has been eaten and even with very young children one can be reasonably certain from the signs and remains around the child. Older persons who suspect that they have eaten something poisonous should tell somebody else or write down the details if they are near to collapse and nobody is around. Slow, insidious, symptoms of ill-health should always be investigated by qualified persons as they may, for instance, indicate an allergy to some common food, quite apart from any suspicion of deliberate poisoning.

The symptoms of poisoning are so variable that diagnosis is difficult unless the previous history is available. Gastrointestinal symptoms, such as vomiting, abdominal pain and diarrhoea are commonly associated with poisoning from a variety of causes. Where the vomit contains berries, seeds or pieces of plant leaf or stem, it should always be retained for examination by a qualified person. It may be the only proof, apart from some vague description which would fit dozens of plants, of the actual plant causing the poisoning. It may be invaluable in predicting the outcome of the poisoning.

Delirium or excitation occur for a variety of reasons, including poisoning by plants. Coma can arise from a variety of causes, a few of which are due to severe plant poisoning. Convulsions occur in a few plant poisonings but are usually due (in the absence of other symptoms) to other causes. Respiratory difficulties occur in some plant poisonings and allergic conditions. Abnormally slow, fast or irregular heartbeat, with associated changes in the strength of the pulse are common in severe plant poisonings. Intense irritation, blistering or burning of the skin or mouth and throat occur with strongly irritant substances.

The first principle of treatment is to remove the patient from the source of his poisoning and to take steps to prevent further absorption of poisons into the body from the digestive system. This means inducing vomiting *as soon as possible* to rid the stomach of residual material, but *only if the patient is conscious*. This is carried out simply, by stimulating the back of the throat with a finger or the handle of a spoon. If possible make the patient drink as much water or milk as he can and then induce vomiting. The old method of making a person vomit by giving them a cup of warm, strong, table salt solution is no longer recommended because in some cases, particularly with young children, the salt itself can cause a dangerous form of poisoning. After the first vomiting repeat the drink and vomiting process a couple of times to clean out the stomach. *Never* induce vomiting if the material eaten or drunk is strongly irritant or corrosive, but instead give a cupful of vegetable (cooking) oil and half to two pints of milk or water. Young children should be laid across the lap when vomiting is being induced, facing downwards with the head lowered over a bowl. This head-lower-than-hips position is desirable for all vomiting as it prevents vomit entering the lungs where even a very small quantity can cause serious or fatal damage. Carry out the whole procedure calmly and without panic.

134

Patients who are gasping for breath or whose breathing has actually stopped should be given artificial respiration at once while someone calls the Emergency Number for skilled help and a breathing apparatus.

A person who has become unconscious, who is in a highly shocked condition, who is going blue (cyanose) or who is having convulsions, should be taken *at once* to a hospital. In coma it is essential to ensure that the air passages are not blocked by saliva or fluids, the patient usually being laid on his side and turned at intervals.

Hospitals and doctors have the equipment to carry out gastric lavage. For this a tube is introduced down the throat into the stomach (taking great care not to get it into the lungs by mistake, which could prove fatal) and tepid water or other suitable liquid or suspension is alternately poured down it and siphoned out again.

The second principle of treatment is to attend to the symptoms and relieve as many as possible of them. It does not matter what the poisonous substance is, it may even be completely unknown. At the hospital, respiratory failure, heart malfunction, convulsions, dehydration, hypothermia and other symptoms will be treated by the appropriate drugs and supportive therapy, a description of which is beyond the scope of this book. Most of these techniques involve complex equipment and potentially dangerous drugs and can only be carried out under the supervision of properly qualified staff who can monitor the effects from minute to minute. In some cases of poisoning it is possible to remove the poison from the blood by means of a dialysis (kidney) machine. In this method the patient's blood is diverted out of the body and 'cleaned'. This has recently been used in treating cases of *Amanita* (pages 114–116) poisoning.

The third principle of treatment is to carry out specific measures to combat the actions of a known poison – the administration of an antidote. Unfortunately there are no real antidotes available, the closest to that ideal being the antiphalloidian serum which is effective if given shortly after symptoms appear in *Amanita phalloides* poisoning. It is prepared by injecting animals with increasing amounts of the toxin from that fungus to produce antibodies in the blood. Very few places have this available, partly because of the scattered and, relatively speaking, rare occurrence of such poisoning. Because of the high fatality in cases of *Amanita* poisoning it still receives considerable attention. Recently, the substance thioctic acid has been mentioned as an effective antidote. Again, it can only be used by qualified staff because special supportive measures are required – otherwise the 'cure' proves fatal – but at least it is more readily available and more easily stored. Other 'antidotes', such as those to *Atropa* (page 72), *Datura* (page 86), *Digitalis* (page 32), *Aconitum* (page 29) and *Nicotiana* (page 110), are merely examples of drugs (often plant-derived) which have the opposite effects to those of the plant causing the poisoning. It is simply matching one poison against another, complementary, one.

4 Allergies

Allergy is defined as a state of increased sensitivity and embodies the idea that only certain, specific members of the human race are actually involved. We can draw a rather hazy distinction between primary irritants, which are in themselves highly toxic substances causing damage directly upon contact, and allergenic susbtances (often in themselves more or less innocuous) which, because of the particular metabolism of certain people, can cause considerable suffering and even death. Many primary irritants, however, can also cause allergic sensitisation.

In allergy the first contact with a substance usually has no visible effect. Changes, however, are set in motion inside the body which cause, in some cases, the production of allergic antibodies or, as they are usually called 'reagins'. These are often considered to be similar to the immune antibodies which protect us from diseases. The reagins, unfortunately, have things the wrong way round. When a second or subsequent contact with the allergenic substance occurs they cause the body to react violently against the allergen. It is this 'unnecessary' reaction which gives rise to the symptoms of allergy.

Doctors usually recognise two types of allergy. In atopic allergy there is usually some clear indication of a hereditary transmission of susceptibility to allergy – not necessarily to the same allergenic substance, but as a general tendency. Also, it is possible to demonstrate the presence in the blood of the reagins for the particular allergenic substance. In non-atopic allergy one or both of these criteria are not met. Many cases of contact dermatitis come within the non-atopic category.

It must be stated, however, that some doctors consider that 'normal' and 'allergic' people merely represent two extremes of a complete spectrum of intershading categories with no clear dividing lines. Likewise, there may be no real, clear-cut distinction between atopic and non-atopic allergies. What may perhaps be more important in the development of the allergic state are such things as the actual nature of the allergen, how much of it enters the body tissues without being inactivated, and how frequently and in what quantities the allergenic material comes into contact with the patient.

For an allergy to develop, the allergenic substance must first come into contact with the body. This contact takes place naturally, either at the skin or the mucous membranes (surface lining the respiratory or digestive systems). It can be anywhere on or in the body – the nose for hay fever, the stomach or intestines for food allergies, the bronchial tubes for asthma, the contact area on the skin for dermatitis. Once the 'shock' tissue has been stimulated it reacts by swelling – either in a localised area or more extensively. This swelling is one of the major causes of the primary symptoms of allergy.

The mechanism of allergy is described in detail on page 139 but, in essence, what happens is that the allergen brings about a reaction with the hypersensitive cells at the site of contact and damages them. This injury causes the tiny blood vessels in the area to increase in diameter, stretching their walls in the process. This makes the walls more porous and blood plasma (the fluid part of the blood) can pass out into the tissues causing them to swell. The site of the reaction is not absolutely fixed, however, and it may be internal (nose, lungs, digestive system) or external (skin) or some variable combination of these depending on the individual. Although the substances which cause the development of an allergy may form a very complex mixture it is normally the protein component, or some chemical (called a haptene) which combines with a protein, which is the actual reactive material.

There are two common systems for the classification of allergens. One is simple and based on the route of sensitisation: inhalant, ingestant, contactant, injectant, infectant. The other is based on the nature of the allergenic substance itself, which often shows some relationship to the occupation or habits of the individual concerned because people in particular industries are exposed to exceptionally high levels of some allergens and hence are more likely to develop an allergy towards them.

Causes of Allergy

In this book we are concerned only with allergenic substances originating from plants and must therefore neglect other causes of allergy, noting only that they can, and frequently do, occur.

Perhaps the easiest plant allergies to understand are those included in the sphere of contact dermatitis. Direct contact with the plant or some product from it gives rise to the allergy. An important aspect in the diagnosis of this form of dermatitis is the pattern of lesions on the affected person. In the absence of other information this can tell us much about the source of the allergenic material. Everyday actions, and many particular industries, bring a person into contact with plants in a very specific manner. In each activity only certain parts of the hands or body actually come into contact with the plant material so the first question which needs to be asked is: what do I touch with that particular part of me? Lesions on the face or legs may easily be related to some outdoor activity involving brushing against plants. The exact pattern on the hands may be more useful because hands come into contact with a multitude of substances, but usually in rather specific ways. Are the areas of contact those used to pick leaves off a pot-plant, to hold a pencil, cut a piece of wood and so on? Nasal or respiratory symptoms clearly indicate a probable airborne source of the allergen.

Inhalent Allergens

The most easily studied type of inhalant allergy is that known as hay fever. Its normally seasonal occurrence points to some environmental change and was easily related to the presence of plant pollen in the air. Plant pollens differ considerably in their properties, the most troublesome plants being wind-pollinated ones, producing large quantities of light pollen, which can drift for long distances. The symptoms of runny nose and eyes with associated itching of the nose, eyes, mouth and even ears have either been seen or experienced by most people.

Rather less obvious is the relationship of allergic asthma since here the symptoms may occur throughout the year with less marked season fluctuations. The breathing difficulties are caused by contraction of the small bronchioles (air passages) in the lungs and a concomitant excess of liquid secretions in the passages. Coughing is an attempt to expel these sticky globules from the lungs. The causes of asthma can often be tracked down to an inhaled dust of plant or other origin.

Symptoms of allergy may also arise from reception through the nasal passages of volatile cosmetic scents and food odours, possibly influenced by psychological mechanisms.

Contactant Allergens

This group includes some of the most obvious examples of allergic responses developing at the site of contact. In other examples the symptoms may be more diffuse and less easily recognised as being due to contact with a particular material. Even where contact is 'obvious' it may take a long time for the person actually afflicted to recognise the true cause of his or her symptoms. Some of the wild and cultivated plants involved have already been described in Chapter 2, or are included on page 153. Numerous plant products are also implicated in contact dermatitis and are listed in Appendix 2 (page 160). Symptoms vary depending on extent of contact; from simple reddening, itching, swellings, tiny or large blisters up to the more permanent ones of skin thickening and cracking. All carry the risks of secondary infection by harmful micro-organisms.

Ingestant/Injectant Allergens

The plant foods commonly involved in allergic responses are dealt with in Chapter 5. The symptoms may arise anywhere along the digestive tract, from lips to anus. Severe reactions consist of vomiting, diarrhoea (blood-stained in some cases), abdominal pains, often general reddening and eruptions on the skin and even death. Apart from the skin reactions and possible proof of allergenicity these symptoms resemble those of many cases of direct poisoning. The symptoms most commonly shown in less severe cases of food allergy include general feelings of ill-health such as depression, weakness, irritability, nervousness, general aches and low fever. Not all symptoms may actually be shown in any one case. Effects in the digestive tract itself may include sore mouth and coated tongue, bad-smelling breath, stomach and intestinal gas (voided by mouth or anus), abdominal pains, diarrhoea or constipation and anal irritation. Sometimes pain may resemble that from forms of ulcer and, in fact, the relationship between food and all manner of digestive upsets may well be an allergic response in more cases than is commonly recognised. Skin eruptions and reddening may occur in some, but by no means all, cases of food allergy.

Among some of the most mysterious allergic responses are 'migraine' type headaches. In some cases these are related to the ingestion of certain foods although the mechanism is still a subject of active scientific research.

Many drugs, both plant derived and otherwise produced, can give rise to allergic symptoms. Even many of the 'wonder drugs' of modern scientific medicine, as well as the 'natural drugs' of other medicinal systems can cause problems due to their allergenicity.

Mechanism of Allergy

The exact interaction which brings about the development of the allergenic state is still not clearly understood although several links in the chain of events have been discovered. The first stages of the chain are the least known. An allergenic substance which has a protein component in it (as have all living plant cells) can bring about the formation of a reagin by a system exactly similar to the normal body defences used to combat infections. It is now thought that some allergenic interactions may involve certain sugar groups (which are highly specific and individual) and that these actually bring about the mutual recognition of the allergen and its reagin or target cell. Whatever the precise system is it brings about a state of sensitisation or hypersensitivity – the ability to respond to further contacts with the allergen.

With these further contacts, one of the first observable changes in the shock tissue is the liberation of histamine from the cells injured by contact with the allergen or its derivatives. Histamine causes a local dilation of the tiny arterioles in the affected area, bringing an enhanced blood supply (causing reddening) to it and at the same time making the capillary walls more permeable to the blood plasma (causing swelling). Although normally the amount of histamine released is only sufficient to cause a localised effect, if the 'injury' is large massive amounts of histamine are produced, entering the blood stream and passing to other parts of the body where they cause similar dilation effects on the blood vessels and leakage of plasma. This may result in loss of consciousness and even death. Some people are more sensitive to a 'shock' (be it allergen or from other causes) than others, and may react abnormally violently, with consequently more serious results.

The liberation of histamine is one of the characteristic ways in which the tissues of a human being react to any form of injury and the same system is set in motion by traumatic (physical injury) and emotional (psychological) stress. This opens the way for complex interactions between allergy, emotion and environment. Not only has some recognisable allergenic substance to be found, but consideration must also be given to the patient's psychological state.

Innumerable cases can be quoted where an emotional stress, of almost any kind, can render more severe an allergenic condition or stimulate it even in the absence of the allergenic substance. In this area we are, of course, on very thin ice, scientifically speaking. Emotion may simply precipitate increased sensitivity to some ubiquitous allergenic substance (of which there are many) but we know that certain forms of allergy cannot be diagnosed by any of the normal methods used to identify allergens. Once again the quantitative nature of allergy must be emphasised – if the symptoms are not great enough to be easily recognised we do not know they exist although the underlying characteristics may well be there, in a 'latent' state.

In the brain there is a normally self-regulating region called the vaso-motor centre. Under rest conditions this is continually sending out signals along the nerves to the capillaries, keeping them in a 'normal' state of contraction. When the nerve impulses are reduced the capillaries swell, an effect which, if extensive, will result in reduction of blood pressure and loss of consciousness. Increasing the number of impulses results in constriction of the peripheral blood vessels, raised blood pressure and preparation of the body for energetic activity by allowing the muscles to receive a greater blood supply.

The vasomotor centre can be influenced by a number of factors, in the present discussion we may note that the higher (thinking) centres of the brain can directly affect its functioning – so the way is open for an emotional effect on capillaries. We have already noted that the tissues in which the capillaries occur can influence the extent of their dilation by means of histamine or some other system.

A further complication arises from the activity of certain hormonal substances in the body. Both adrenalin (from the adrenal glands) and pituitrin (from the pituitary gland) cause contraction of the small blood vessels and they are produced in greater amounts under some conditions of stress. Also active upon the walls of the blood vessels, tending to decrease their porosity, are the substances cortisone and, indirectly, adrenocorticotrophic hormone (ACTH). Straightforward physical influences like light and heat tend to dilate the surface capillaries while cold tends to contract them.

The normal maintenance of the correct tone in the blood vessels is mainly due to the activity of the sympathetic nervous system. Stimulation of the para-sympathetic nervous systems found in the skin causes the liberation of acetylcholine. This in its turn can cause the liberation of vasodilating substances such as bradykinin and hence lead to the allergic response.

Certain mutually antagonistic biochemical changes are also involved in the reactions of both these nervous systems. Both operate below the level of conscious thought but this does not mean to say that they are unaffected by emotional factors. In fact, as has frequently been demonstrated, what may at first be a perfectly straightforward case of allergy to contact with some specific substance, can easily develop into the situation where mere sight of the allergenic material (such as some particular item of food) will bring on the absolutely real symptoms of allergy, just as if actual contact had occurred.

140

Treatment

Two basic methods are available for the specific treatment of allergy. Firstly the obvious, if not always easy, method is to avoid contact with the allergen once it has been specifically identified. Secondly, an attempt can be made to reduce the level of sensitivity of the body to the allergen – a process known as hyposensitisation. The remaining techniques merely involve treating or alleviating the symptoms once they have occurred.

Before considering specific treatments we must discuss the way in which the identity of the allergen is established.

The plants known to cause allergies have already been outlined and are listed in Appendix 2. How do we set about finding the causative agent? A detailed case history is vitally important – perhaps even a minute-by-minute diary extending over days, weeks or years. The aim is to link cause and effect – what actions preceded the attack of allergic symptoms. The area of contact is clearly a starting point. Many parts of the body, however, come into contact with a host of possible allergenic substances. So we ask many questions. Did you do any gardening? Enter a greenhouse? Visit friends? Water the pot-plants? Prepare a vase of flowers? And so on, almost *ad infinitum*. Many people, of course, don't recall the really significant events because these are commonplace actions. Many even deny possessing particular potted plants – even when the doctor can see one himself on a home visit!

As a result of the case-history the doctor may decide on an attempt to actually identify the allergen by specific tests. This is normally a job for the specialist and rarely undertaken outside of special clinics and hospitals, for two reasons. Firstly it requires specialised reagents and trained staff and secondly there is an element of danger in it – very small if the correct facilities are to hand, but possibly serious if they are not and the reaction to the allergen is exceptionally violent. Unfortunately there are no really satisfactory 'in vitro' (test-tube) tests for the presence of skin-sensitising reagins. In most cases they fail to bring about any recognisable precipitation reaction, which is a normal method for detecting the ordinary immune antibodies. One method which has been used is to detect the liberation of histamine from white blood cells taken from the allergic person. But, as mentioned previously, many patients do not have any recognisable form of reactive antibody in their blood. So we come to the direct skin testing upon the patient.

Basically the system is simple. The suspected material or an extract from it is applied either to the undamaged surface of the skin (patch or scratch test) or injected just below the skin surface (intradermal test). The former is commonly carried out on the back of limbs, wherever an extensive area of readily observable and not too hairy skin is present. The intradermal test should never be carried out anywhere except on the arm because the greater contact of allergen and body tissues may result in serious reactions needing immediate isolation (for example by torniquet) of the injection area, and supportive measures.

Skin testing is not, however, as simple as it may sound. There are many thousands of substances which can bring about a skin reaction. About a thousand different actual preparations for skin testing are available. Obviously it would be impossible to try them all out so they are grouped together into diagnostic groups. When the group has been identified, the actual substance can be more easily located within it. Many variations of the actual testing procedure exist, designed to cut out such factors as the possibility of reaction to the tape used to cover the test, to improve reliability and so on. The age and physical condition of the patient can influence the response, as well as even the time of year when the test is carried out. This may be due to a general increase in sensitivity brought about by contact with a common allergen such as pollen. In the tests cross-reactions are common. A person may respond to chemically similar substances or to the extracts from botanically related plants. Frequently, a botanical relationship also includes a chemical one. The converse situation can exist, however, in which only certain cultivars of the same species may be allergenic. More commonly, as with *Primula* allergy, different species show variation in allergenicity.

Once specific causes of allergy have been identified the necessary steps can be taken to remove them or isolate the patient from them. If it is food, don't eat it. If it is a plant in the house or garden, get rid of it. If it is something at one's place of work or in one's leisure activities these must be changed, or protective clothing, including perhaps gloves or mask, worn. Where this remedy is not possible a course of hyposensitisation may be carried out. This is most frequently undertaken for inhalent allergens such as pollen, house-dust or other airborne particles. Its use in contact allergies, such as that caused by poison ivy is open to considerable criticism and has strong antagonists as well as strong protagonists. Briefly, the technique of hyposensitisation is to raise the level of allergen to which the body responds with definite symptoms, until this threshold is above the commonly encountered levels of contact. The course of treatment starts with a very low level of an extract of the allergenic material and progresses slowly to increasing doses as the body system becomes more tolerant of the presence of the allergen. This may take some time – an excessive dose given too soon will precipitate the symptoms that the doctor is trying to prevent. Skin tests are used frequently to check the level of sensitivity before moving on to the next higher dosage. Eventually, only occasional booster injections may be necessary to keep the allergy under control.

Non-specific therapy can be used whether or not the actual allergen has been identified. It seeks only to alleviate the symptoms and its principles are simple. Earlier in the chapter a discussion of the mechanism of the allergic response was given. Treatment consists in trying to prevent or reverse any of the systems which are operative. Obviously, if the doctor suspects emotional problems as a contributory cause these must be tackled in the appropriate manner. In any case, the treatment of all but the simplest allergies is a prolonged process and clearly needs the full co-operation of the patient.

Drug therapy is used in three ways. Firstly, to alleviate immediate symptoms while the case is being investigated; secondly to assist the patient who has developed symptoms caused by some known contact with the allergen;

thirdly to ease the symptoms of patients where no more specific remedy can be found. Clearly, one can use more powerful drugs on sporadic allergies than one can (because of possible harmful long-term effects) on a continuous allergic situation.

The action of the sympathetic nervous system can be simulated by the sympatheticomimetic drugs which produce constriction of the blood vessels and thereby reduce swelling and symptoms. In this group are several well-known substances. Various preparations of adrenaline (epinephrine) are used, some for rapid release by injection, others for slow release. Nebulisers (atomisers) for oral spraying may also be used. Adrenaline is a natural substance produced by the human body but it can still give rise to such adverse symptoms as dizziness, headache and restlessness. Ephedrine comes from the plant *Ephedra vulgaris* and is similar to adrenaline but with a more prolonged, less severe activity and the advantage that it can be taken orally as a medicinal preparation. It may also be used in a nebuliser. Once again, side effects similar to those from adrenaline may occur. Some relief from these may be obtained by using sedatives or hypnotics at the same time. Several synthetic chemicals, some related to ephedrine have often been used instead of the natural drugs. These include such well-known compounds as 'Benzedrine'. Ergotamine is sometimes used for its constrictive effect on blood vessels and seems particularly popular for the treatment of allergies in which migraine occurs – but not, of course, during pregnancy. Sometimes included in the present category are drugs like caffeine and aminophylline which provide some relief by dilating the bronchioles in allergic asthma, but have negligible effect on other allergic conditions.

In theory, drugs which inhibit the parasympathetic nervous system should also be useful in the treatment of allergies. In practice they are less effective and are usually used in combinations with other drugs. Atropine (or the less pure belladonna) is of benefit particularly in alleviating allergic symptoms in the intestines, or nose and eyes. Once again side effects such as dilation of the pupils of the eye, blurred vision, dry mouth and so on may occur. *Hyoscyamus* is of similar benefit for intestinal allergies. Stramonium has been used for years in the treatment of asthma, usually by burning a mixture of the powder from the herb *Datura stramonium* and saltpetre. The fumes are said to be beneficial. Many other forms of smoking mixtures are available for asthmatics. Although they may be helpful to some people they are generally poorly thought of by the medical profession – if for no other reason than the fact that some people get even more severe symptoms from the so-called cure.

Although narcotics such as cocaine, pethidine and codeine are occasionally used in the treatment of intractible allergies, they are not to be recommended due to the danger of addiction with many of them. This can easily result in a drug-dependent emotionally-triggered allergic response of no benefit to anyone.

Since histamine is a key substance in the development of the allergic response it is reasonable that antihistamine drugs should find a place in therapy. A large number of chemicals are available, differing in potency and in the various adverse side-effects they produce. Prolonged use of any of them leads to tolerance and hence to loss of effectiveness. Many of the more effective antihistamines have an additional sedative action. Many other side effects, such as insomnia, nervousness, blurred vision, gastro-intestinal symptoms and so on may occur and must be watched for so that if they become severe a new drug can be tried. Frequently used drugs in this group are the hydrochlorides of diphenhydramine, tripelennamine, and promethazine. Some antihistamines are used for allergic symptoms on the skin as well as for inhalant allergies.

Mention has already been made of the role of hormones in allergy and a commonly used treatment involves preparations containing corticosteroids. Therapy with these hormones however is always a calculated risk, since supplying the body with additional quantities of hormone can upset the natural regulating systems of the body. Excessive use will result in the symptoms of Cushing's disease: moon face, skin fragility, decreased resistance to infections and so on. Other possibly related reactions, seen during the steroid therapy of some people, include personality changes, diabetes, ulcers and many more. The dangers of these various side-effects are clearly greater with continuous treatment using large doses of steroids over long periods. The natural hormones cortisone and hydrocortisone are often used as well as a wide range of synthetic compounds with rather similar activities. In other cases ACTH, the pituitary hormone which stimulates the body's own production of corticosteroids may be used in place of the cortico-steroids themselves. The most commonly used forms of steroid therapy are for skin application, in various types of cream base, with or without other active ingredients. Oral doses may also be given, but injections are rarely used unless the allergy is producing widespread bodily symptoms.

5 Harmful Substances in Food

There are three main ways in which food, eaten in good faith, can produce harmful effects in the person eating it. Firstly, where the raw foodstuff contains harmful substances which would be removed by proper preparation or cooking of the food. In some cases eating a well-known food in an unusual way can cause trouble. Dietary patterns and eating habits often vary from one country to another. Methods of preparation based on experience may occasionally be forgotten when new foodstuffs travel across national frontiers. With several common food plants, of course, only certain parts of the plant can be consumed. Eat other parts and the result can be a case of dangerous poisoning. The occasional but highly dangerous use of rhubarb leaves in a salad or as a vegetable is one example.

A second group of harmful foods are those which cause allergies in certain people. The response here is typical of the allergic reaction: most people can consume the food with equanimity while the unfortunate few suffer symptoms ranging from 'mild distress' to 'acute discomfort'.

A third way in which trouble can arise is by 'food-poisoning' caused by micro-organisms getting into or onto food, perhaps even multiplying within it. This is, to a large extent, the domain of 'food science' with its distinct disciplines of hygiene, preparation, preservation and so on. In the home, prevention is largely a question of possessing a basic knowledge of the causes of food poisoning and acting accordingly. Usually this means correctly storing, cooking and handling food.

It is not my purpose, in this book, to consider the harmful effect, if any, which can arise from food containing 'permitted' preservatives, additives, colouring agents and so on; nor to discuss the merits of 'natural' as against 'synthetic' foodstuffs. I merely wish to draw the reader's attention to dangers which can exist in food.

Toxic Components Found Naturally in Foodstuffs

As we have already seen (page 132), food is that material which we place in our mouth, usually breaking it up into smaller pieces with our teeth (if present!), and which then passes by reflex muscular action into the stomach. The stomach is provided with an inlet valve which normally allows the food to pass only into the stomach but which can, due to a variety of different causes – among them the swallowing of certain noxious substances – allow the food to be regurgitated. Being sick is a common means of ridding the digestive system of harmful substances which have been swallowed. Under these conditions it is clearly a very beneficial process, only to be prevented if the harmful substance is actively corrosive and would cause further damage as it passed upwards through the oesophagous.

Food, depending on its type, consists of variable proportions of the basic components – carbohydrates, fats and proteins. Most people can digest, more or less completely, the proteins and fats and part of the carbohydrates. The main non-digestible carbohydrate is cellulose, which forms a fairly high proportion of natural plant foodstuffs. It provides bulk, or roughage, in the diet.

In man the non-digested part of the food passes out of the body as faeces. The various parts of the human digestive system perform different functions and the various components in the food are predominantly broken down in different parts of the tract. In brief, large molecules in the food are degraded, by special proteins called enzymes, to smaller ones which can then be absorbed through the walls, particularly of the small intestine. The digestive system also contains micro-organisms – the so-called 'gut flora' – which may help or hinder the digestive processes. In diarrhoea the food components may pass through the system so rapidly that not all the nutrients have time to be fully absorbed by the gut. Also water, normally absorbed towards the end of the tract, is not reabsorbed as much as it should be.

Apart from the three major components, food also contains various essential vitamins, minerals and other trace components which are absorbed as the food passes through the system. Dozens of other, non-nutrient substances occur in food and may or may not be absorbed by the digestive tract according to their nature. We are concerned here with substances which either upset normal digestion or are harmful when absorbed by the gut, remembering, of course, that too much of even perfectly wholesome foods – particularly fatty, spicy or sugary ones – can cause mild digestive upsets. Exceptional among foods, or perhaps one should say delicacies since it is not widely eaten, is the fungus *Coprinus atramentarius* (ink cap). When consumed on its own there are no ill effects, but if alcoholic drinks are also taken a distinct reddening of the face and body occurs within a couple of hours. Pulse rate increases and the afflicted person feels distinctly warm. In due course the symptoms wear off as the alcohol is eliminated from the system, but too rapid a return to the evil drink causes a return of the symptom until the fungal substances have lost their effectiveness.

Inhibitors of Normal Digestion

One of the most investigated aspects of food toxicity concerns foods which contain substances that inhibit the normal processes of digestion. When proteins are eaten they are broken down into their simple components – the amino acids – by enzymes called 'proteases'. Many plants contain substances which inhibit the digestion of proteins. Most often it is the seed which causes problems; in particular soybeans and many legume seeds. It has been suggested that the inhibiting substances may help the plants to build up reserves of protein in their storage organs or may stunt the growth of insects which eat seeds containing the inhibitors. As far as man and other animals are concerned much information is available about the effects on nutrition. Unfortunately, many of the results are somewhat contradictory. What is clear, however, is that soybeans will not support the good growth of animals unless they have been well cooked before feeding. Soybeans, it should be noted, contain a very high percentage of protein and should make an excellent food – indeed they do when well cooked. Cooking easily removes the inhibitors contained in soybeans. Fifteen minutes steaming removes nearly all and greatly improves the beans' nutritional value.

Experiments have shown that soybeans contain substances which directly inhibit the action of digestive enzymes, such as trypsin, which break down proteins. It would appear that eating raw soybeans would stop the proper digestion of food and lead to a shortage of amino acids. This simple, direct, explanation is probably not true. More detailed studies suggest that the pancreas is stimulated to overactivity by the inhibitors, causing a more rapid loss of amino acids from the body. The result is a shortage of amino acids, particularly those such as methionine and cystine, in which the soybeans protein itself is deficient. Adding these and other amino acids to the diet often overcomes the harmful effects of raw soybeans. Cooking, of course, is much cheaper! Nutritional problems are often very difficult to solve to the scientists' satisfaction. Soybeans also contain other inhibitors of growth which may act in alternative ways, thereby obscuring the problem.

Of the many other plant seeds which can cause problems similar to raw soybeans the various species of 'beans' need mentioning and the reader's attention is drawn to some of the names given on page 148. Cooking of most sorts of beans is recommended.

Raw peanuts are also known to contain a powerful enzyme inhibitor and extracts from them have even been used to slow down the too-rapid dissolution of blood clots which occurs in hemophiliacs. This inhibitor seems quite stable to heat as it can be extracted even from roasted peanuts. There seem to be few reports of harm from eating too many peanuts – perhaps nobody eats enough for this to show.

Cereal grains are also known to contain inhibitors and beneficial effects have been obtained in animal feeding trials by heating wheat germ. The level of inhibitor is so low, however, that some scientists doubt if it could have any significant effect, even when eaten raw.

Potato tubers contain substances which will inhibit a wide range of enzymes breaking down proteins. Little is known of their significance in nutrition and in any case potatoes are usually cooked before being eaten.

Mention should be made of the various 'synthetic' meats made out of isolated soybean protein by a variety of processes. As eaten, most of these seem to be reasonably free from growth-inhibiting substances, probably as a result of the various purification stages used in their manufacture and cooking.

Some foods containing inhibitors of digestive enzymes. This is not of any great significance unless the diet is very unbalanced

Botanical Name	Common Name
Seeds	
Arachis hypogeae	peanut, ground nut
Artocarpus integrifolia	jack fruit
Avena sativa	oats
Cajanus cajan	red gram
Cajanus indicus	pigeon peas
Canavalia ensiformis	jack bean
Ceratonia siligua	carob bean
Cicer arietinum	chick pea, Bengal gram
Dolichos lablab	field or hyacinth bean
Faba vulgaris	double bean
Fagopyrum esculentum	buckwheat
Gleditsia tricanthus	honey locust
Glycine max	soybean
Hordeum vulgare	barley
Lens culinaris	lentil
Medicago sativa	alfalfa
Oryza sativa	rice
Phaseolus aureus	green gram, mung bean
Phaseolus coccineus	scarlet runner bean
Phaseolus lunatus	butter or Lima bean
Phaseolus mungo	black gram
Phaseolus vulgaris	kidney, French, black, haricot, navy, pinto, white or wax bean
Pisum sativum	garden or field pea
Secale cereale	rye
Triticum vulgare	wheat
Vicia faba	broad, horse or fava bean
Vigna unguiculata	cow or black-eyed pea
Zea mays	maize, sweetcorn or corn
Roots	
Beta vulgaris	beet or beetroot
Brassica rapa	turnip
Colocasia esculenta	taro
Ipomoea battata	yam or sweet potato
Solanum tuberosum	white potato or potato

A Dose of Cyanide

Traces of cyanide, in a combined form, occur in many plants. A few plants contain concentrations which, when liberated, can be considered dangerous. Perhaps the most familiar is the substance amygdalin found in bitter almonds and many other seeds such as apple, prune, plum, peach, cherry, pear, apricot, lemon and lime. Intentional eating of any of these, on a large scale, is not recommended. The occasional 'pip' swallowed does little harm.

The substance called linamarin occurs especially in dark-seeded types of the Lima bean, in cassava and in flax. A nineteenth-century account of bean poisoning describes the symptoms as severe abdominal pains, vomiting and finally the typical symptoms of cyanide poisoning. Poisoning by cassava, a staple part of the diet in many parts of the world, is prevented by its proper preparation. Liberation of the cyanide from its combined forms readily occurs when the plant is handled and washed in water. The cyanide comes out of the food and can be washed or boiled off. Inadequate washing or cooking with a lid on can result in poisoning. That eastern delicacy, bamboo shoots, is another potent source of cyanide. Normally most of this is lost by proper preparation due to the action of the plants own enzymes.

What happens to ingested cyanide-liberating substances is not clearly understood. In some cases the micro-organisms normally present in the gut may liberate cyanide.

How to prevent cyanide poisoning by food is fairly obvious. Those foods which contain and liberate cyanide must be properly prepared for eating. A legislative procedure adopted by some countries prevents the use by humans of food containing more than a certain limit of cyanide-producing substances. In practice, this is usually achieved by the selective breeding of cultivars low in cyanogenic substances. This should prevent outright poisoning. In many tropical countries, however, a slow chronic, poisoning may occur due to persistent intake of low levels of cyanide, linked with generally poor nutrition. Such possibilities are difficult to prove or disprove.

It's in the Blood

Several foods contain substances known to act on the blood. One of the most unusual is the syndrome known as favism – a term first used in the late nineteenth century by an Italian doctor. When certain people eat broad beans or inhale the pollen of this plant they develop a serious anemia due to a breakdown of their red blood cells (hemolysis). Eating uncooked beans gives the most severe reactions. Symptoms appear a few minutes after inhaling the pollen or a few hours after eating the beans. Usually the patient recovers spontaneously after a few days but deaths can occur, especially in young children.

Although broad beans are grown all over the world only certain areas, particularly in the Mediterranean region, are subject to severe favism. The reason for this was not understood until unrelated research on a hereditary sensitivity to a drug, which also caused hemolysis, gave the clue to the nature of favism. In 1956 W. H. Crosby made the essential analogy which was soon supported by experimental evidence. Different ethnic groups had differing occurrences of a deficiency of an enzyme called glucose-6-phosphate dehydrogenase (G6PD for short). Many Mediterranean peoples and American negroes, among others, had a particularly high incidence of this enzyme defect. Where favism occurred it was linked to the G6PD deficiency. However, not all G6PD deficient races show favism so once again the answer is not simple – some people are more deficient than others! Knowledge is hampered by lack of suitable experimental systems but some factor outside the red blood cells themselves is indicated by the results available.

When red blood cells are treated with substances called saponins, they are hemolysed. The saponins have in common the ability to form stable, soap-like foams. Certain primitive tribes have used them to kill fish, by placing saponin-containing plant material in the water. When eaten by man such fish are non-toxic and it is generally agreed that saponins are quite harmless to humans. They do, in fact, form an important component in certain food products, acting as a foaming agent. Plants which contain natural saponins – such as spinach, sugarbeet, asparagus and beetroot – are not known to cause any problems. Any saponins present in food seem to be absorbed only poorly and even if they do enter the blood it has been found that the red blood cells are protected from their toxic effects by the blood plasma which is present.

Many plants, particularly those belonging to the legume and euphorbia families, contain substances which cause red blood cells to stick together (agglutinate). Such substances are known as lectins or phytohemagglutinins. Although some of the plants containing lectins are among the most poisonous known, such as *Abrus* and *Ricinus*, others are common foodstuffs like beans. These rarely give trouble except when eaten only partially cooked and in large amounts. The problem is, however, sufficiently serious to limit the use of bean flour to products which are subjected to moist rather than dry cooking. In some cases it may be accompanying substances rather than the lectin itself which causes trouble. The poisonous nature of castor beans has already been mentioned (page 49) and they should never be used as a purgative substitute for the purified castor oil.

Pea Disease

Human neurolathyrism is characterised by spinal cord degeneration and consequent loss of use of the legs. Unfortunately it occurs as a serious health problem in countries where consumption of the seeds of species of *Lathyrus*, such as the chick pea, is prevalent. The sweet pea (*Lathyrus odoratus*) is poisonous but the component known to be present in sweet pea – (beta-gamma-L-glutamyl) aminopropionitrile – does not occur in the chick pea. This substance, in fact, gives rise to a totally different skeletal effect, called osteolathyrism. Even Hippocrates was aware that certain peas were toxic but sadly the effects are still seen in Europe, Africa and especially India.

Although the active substance causing neurolathyrism has not been fully identified, attention has been focused upon certain amino acids which have definite neurotoxic properties. Symptoms usually appear after several months on a diet containing a high percentage of chick peas, and take the form of

150

weakness, paralysis of the legs and even death. The obvious solution of stopping the cultivation of lathyrogenic plants is, unfortunately, not possible, largely due to economic and social factors. The seeds do, in fact, have quite a good quality protein content. If cooked in an excess of water which is subsequently drained off, or if soaked in water, most of the toxic substance is removed. The methods used to prepare certain types of unleavened bread, however, do not remove any significant amount of the toxin. Different cooking procedures would do much, therefore, to improve the problem. Planting only varieties which are naturally low in toxin would also help. No known cure exists once the symptoms have developed.

Enlargement of the Thyroid

The enlargement of the thyroid, also known as goitre, usually occurs as a result of a deficiency of iodine in the diet. Certain plants contain substances which can give rise to an enlargement of the thyroid; in particular, the thioglucosides present in cabbage, mustard, turnips, horseradish and radish. In some of these it is actually the thioglucosides which gives the plant its desirable flavour.

Although experimental feeding to animals gives rise to goitre there is considerable doubt as to whether or not these plants are ever the cause of goitre in humans. In most cases the quantity consumed is too small to have a significant effect. This does not mean, however, that they can be neglected. New methods of processing, or new foods, might well result in increased amounts of goitrogenic substance. Some scientists consider that the feeding of large amounts of *Brassica* greens to cows can result in the passage of goitrogenic substances into the milk and hence into humans. Other workers, however, do not consider this as a serious cause of goitre.

Apart from the thioglucosides mentioned above, other goitrogenic substances are suspected in the skins of seeds such as the peanut and cashew nut. Such substances are not well-known but seem unlikely to cause any problems in a normal diet.

Food Allergies

The old saying 'one man's meat is another man's poison' applies quite literally to food allergy. Some people can eat all manner of foods with impunity. Others have only to consume a small quantity of a certain food to precipitate a drastic reaction. The general aspects of allergic reaction have already been discussed in Chapter 4. Allergic reactions to food often have a hereditary basis and are also difficult to study because the effects can rarely be demonstrated in laboratory animals – those poor creatures 'beloved' by toxicologists.

The effects of allergy to food may reveal themselves in a wide variety of ways. Skin reactions and respiratory problems are commonly found. Actually direct effects on the gut are rare, but when they do occur they can mimic serious medical conditions. Severe headache (migraine) can result from some foods. Great attention should be paid, indirectly, to children who complain of vague pains or digestive upsets after eating certain foods. This may well indicate an allergy to a particular food rather than sheer awkwardness! Unfortunately many cases of food allergy are extremely difficult to pinpoint and eradicate. The parent in the home often has a better chance of finding the cause, through a knowledge of day-to-day diet and health changes, than the doctor has in a few minutes in his surgery. In suspected cases complete removal of a particular food for a period of weeks may help confirm one's suspicions or dispose of one's fears.

Often the offending substance may appear to have little effect on the gut itself but instead will give rise to skin eruptions or respiratory symptoms. Rapid reactions are usually the most dangerous. Those which take several hours to develop usually also pass away without too many problems. Some reactions may be so slight as to be barely noticed until a change of diet brings about a feeling of better health. Eating irritant foods such as onions, radish and spices may exacerbate a normally mild reaction. Actual positive identification of a food allergy will be based on the various objective and subjective tests mentioned in connection with allergies in general (Chapter 4).

Although allergies tend to be rather personal affairs and long lists can be prepared covering all manner of foodstuffs, there are certain foods which give problems more often than others. In most cases the actual allergenic substance appears to be mainly a protein, although it may actually only form a very small part of the food itself. The amount and nature of the substance may change during the various stages of development of a plant, during storage, processing and food preparation and even perhaps during digestion itself. Some allergens are stable to heat, others rapidly destroyed by heating.

Wheat, and any product made from it such as bread, is a common allergen. Usually this allergic effect is picked up when an infant is put onto 'solid' food since most of these contain some form of wheat flour. Related cereals such as maize can also have similar effects. Rice is often used as an alternative to wheat when an allergy to the latter exists. Rice can, however, produce allergies itself, particularly if used in the 'natural' or 'unpolished' state. Other alternatives such as rye and barley can also, on occasion, cause allergies. Perhaps the best substitute, since it only rarely causes allergy, is the oat. The allergic reaction to the non-cereal buckwheat has already been mentioned (page 65).

All manner of vegetables and legumes can cause allergic responses which may differ widely, in any one person, according to the different types which can be eaten. Raw vegetables may often be allergenic while the cooked product is harmless. Peanuts are often quoted as one of the most allergenic legumes but many peas and beans can provoke trouble. Some people are highly allergic to soybeans in any form.

Among the fruits, strawberries are a frequently quoted cause of allergy. This is usually easily overcome by cooking or even surface-blanching with boiling water. Bananas, pineapples, mangos and other tropical fruits may all cause problems.

Nuts and seeds, or products from them such as mustard, flavourings and spices, can all provoke violent reactions. Even the sesame, caraway or poppy seeds on bakery products can be harmful. Products from seeds, such as chocolate, have been instrumental in allergic reactions, particularly migraine. Almost any drink can, but fortunately only rarely does, provoke an allergic response.

In conclusion, any food may cause an allergy and only one member of a family may be affected. Common sense and a little observation should help one to keep away from foods which do not agree with self, family or friends. Many an unpleasant evening can be saved if one makes the habit of enquiring what suits one's guests before serving it up to them!

Some foods commonly causing allergic responses. Cooking reduces allergenicity in all cases

Group	Substance	Notes
Cereals	barley	Frequently causes allergy directly and in the form of malt extracts
	buckwheat	Used in some foods, can be highly allergenic
	corn (maize)	Common allergen
	oats	Good alternative to wheat and corn, not commonly allergenic
	rice	Often used as an alternative to wheat and corn but also can be allergenic
	rye	Often used as an alternative but can be allergenic
	wheat	very common allergen
Vegetables	asparagus	
	beans, peas	All types
	cabbage	
	carrots	
	cauliflower	
	celery	
	potato	
	soybeans	
	squash	
	turnip	
Fruits	apple	
	apricot	
	banana	
	canteloupe	
	fig	
	grapefruit	
	lemon	
	lime	
	mango	May be due to surface contamination with sap

	orange	
	peach	
	raspberries	
	strawberries	
Nuts	all types of nut and any products containing nuts	
Salads	cucumber	
	green salads	Rare
	radish	
	tomato	
Herbs, spices, condiments, flavourings	anise	All these are rarely allergenic but can be severely so on occasion
	bay	
	caraway	
	cinnamon	
	clove	
	flavouring oils	
	ginger	
	mustard	
	nutmeg	
	parsley	
	pepper	
	poppy	
	sage	
	sesame	Seeds used in bakery products
	thyme	
	vanilla	
Fungi	moulds	Types used in cheeses
	mushrooms	
	yeast	Can cause severe reaction in any form (bread, health food etc)
Processed	chocolate	
	cocoa butter	
	cocoa/coffee	Not highly allergenic due to temperature treatments
	pasta	Macaroni, spaghetti etc
Oils	almond	Highly purified oils are not very allergenic
	coconut	
	cottonseed	Used in mayonnaise and sardine oil
	flax seed	Used in bakery products
	peanut	
Vegetable gums	acacia	Used in ice cream, icings, diabetic foods, milk desserts etc
	karaya	
	tragacanth	

Appendix 1 Some plants reported as poisonous to man (see Chapters 2 and 3)

The grouping into sections is a personal choice since in many cases the poisonous substances occur throughout the plants. Reference codes are detailed at the end.

Scientific Name	Common Name	Notes	Reference
Fungi			
Agaricus meleagris			Z
A. xanthoderma	yellow-staining mushroom	Enteritis	N
Boletus pachypus			H
B. satanus	devil's boletus	Enteritis	N
Clathrus columnatus	lattice fungus	Convulsions and stupor	K
Claviceps purpurea	ergot	Contaminant in food	N
Cortinarius orellanus			Z
Hebeloma crustuliniforme	poison pie	Enteritis	N
Hypholoma fasiculare	sulphur tuft		N
Lactarius spp	milk caps	Enteritis, may be fatal	H
Paxillus involutus		Harmless when cooked	L
Pholiota autumnalis		Fatal	K
Psilocybe spp		Hallucinogenic, perhaps fatal	K
Ramaria formosa	handsome clavaria	Purging	N
Russula spp	sickener	Enteritis if not cooked	N
Stropharia spp	verdigris agaric, etc.		H
Tricholoma tigrinum	spotted tricholoma	Enteritis	N
Tricholoma spp	various		H
Seeds			
Aquilegia vulgaris	columbine	May be fatal	N
Areca catechu	betel nut	May be fatal	HA
Arecastrum romanzoffianum	coco plum		D
Argemone mexicana	Mexican poppy	Contaminant in food, alkaloids	K
Asagraea spp	sabadilla	Veratrine	O

Avicennia nitida	black mangrove		D
Caesalpina gilliesii	bird of paradise		O
Cassia occidentalis	coffee weed	Laurotetanine, may be fatal	D
Castanospermum australe	moreton bay chestnut	Saponin	D
Caulophyllum thalictroides	blue cohosh		O
Cercis canadensis	redbud tree		O
Cytisus spp	brooms		O
Daubentonia spp	wild macaw plant		O
Dolichos lablab	hyacinth bean	Cyanogenic, unless well cooked	HA
Erythrina herbacea	red cardinal	Alkaloids, hypnotic	D
Erythrina spp	coral tree	Used in seed beads	O
Gossypium spp	cotton	Pigment gossypol	K
Hedysarum mackenzii	wild sweet pea		O
Helenium tenuifolium	sneezeweed	Contaminant in food	K
Illicium anisatum	star anise		D
Ipomoea spp	morning glory	Hallucinogenic	O
Lathyrus odoratus	sweet pea		D
Lathyrus spp	peas		K
Lupinus spp	lupins	Alkaloids	N
Malus sylvestris	apple	Cyanogenetic glycoside	K
Mimosa spp	mimosa		O
Mirabilis jalapa	four-o-clock	May be fatal	O
Nepeta cataria	catnip		O
Phaseolus lunatus	Lima bean	Cyanogenetic glycoside	K
P. coccineus	scarlet runner bean	Possibly toxic	K
Physostigma venenosia	calabar bean	Fatal	O
Pongamia pinnata	pongam	Pongamiin	D
Psoralea argophylla	scurf pea		K
Quercus spp	oaks	Tannins?	K
Saponaria spp	soap berry etc	Saponins	K
Senecio spp	groundsels, ragworts	Contaminant in food	D
Stizolobium deeringianum	velvet bean		K
Strelitzia spp	bird-of-paradise	Enteritis	HA
Strophanthus spp	strophanthus		D
Tephrosia spp	tephrosia	Tephrosin, may be fatal	D
Thermopsis rhombifolia	false lupine	Alkaloids	K
Vicia faba	broad bean	Genetically linked hepatitis	K
Various species of *Cycas*	cycads	May be used as food	K

Fruits

Allamanda cathartica	yellow allamanda	Used as cathartic	K
Calophyllum inophyllum	mast wood		D
Citrullus colocynthis	bitter apple	Colocynth, may be fatal	D
Diospyros virginiana	American persimmon	Tannins may form phytobezoars	D
Ecballium elaterium	squirting cucumber	Elaterin	D

Eschscholtzia spp	poppy		O
Ficus spp	rubber tree, fig		O
Guaiacum officinale	lignum vitae	Resin is toxic	HA
Momordica spp	balsam apple		O
Morus rubra	red mulberry	Unripe fruit and leaf sap	HA
Ochrosia elliptica	ochrosia plum		HA
Philadelphus spp	mock orange	May be fatal	O
Solanum aculeatissimum	devil's apple		K
Urechites spp	yellow nightshade	Heart failure possible	HA

Berries

Aglaonema spp	Chinese water-evergreen		O
Andromeda spp		Andromedotoxin	O
Celastrus scandens	bittersweet	Celastrin	O
Cestrum nigrum	night-blooming jasmine	Solanine	O
Cocculus indicus		May be fatal	O
Cotoneaster spp	cotoneaster		O
Crateagus spp	hawthorn		O
Ilex aquifolium	holly	Vomiting and purge	N
Ilex spp	cassena etc		D
Lonicera spp	honeysuckles		O
Nicandra spp	apple of Peru		O
Paris quadrifolia	herb paris	Saponin, paristyphnin	N
Polygonatum spp	solomon's seal	Anthraquinone	N
Pyrocantha spp	firethorn	Vomiting	O
Rhodotypos spp	jet bead bush	May be fatal	O
Sorbus spp	mountain ash		N

Underground Parts

Amaryllis belladonna	belladonna lily	Belladonine	D
Arnica montana	leopard's bane	May cause coma	HA
Aspidium filix-mas	male fern	Folk-medicine, may be fatal	O
Cocculus ferrandianus	moonseed	Alkaloids	O
Cyclamen spp	cyclamen	May be fatal	O
Derris elliptica	derris	Fatal in some cases	O
Endymion nonscriptus	blue bell		N
Erythronium spp	adder's tongue	Violent vomiting	O
Fritillaria meleagris	snake's head fritillary	Alkaloids	N
Gladiolus spp	gladiolus	Vomiting	O
Gloriosa spp	climbing lilies	May be fatal	O
Hyacinthus orientalis	hyacinth	Has poisoned animals	K
Iris spp	iris	Burning sensation	O
Lilium tigrinum	tiger lily	Vomiting	O
Manihot esculenta	cassava	Cyanogenic unless cooked	HA
Ornithogalum spp	snowdrop	Alkaloid	K
Polygala senega	snakeroot	Source of irritant drug	K
Sanguinaria canadensis	bloodroot	Alkaloids	K
Scilla spp	bluebells		O
Spigelia marilandica	indiana pink	May be fatal, as vermifuge	O

Tulipa spp	tulip		N
Yucca spp	spanish bayonet	May be fatal	O
Zamia spp	coontie, florida arrow root	Cyanogenetic glycoside	D
Zephyranthes atamasco	rain lily	Has poisoned animals	K

Leaves

Alocasia macrorrhiza	ape	Calcium oxalate? Raw	O
Antirrhinum spp	snapdragon	Purgative	O
Asclepias spp	milkweed		O
Begonia spp	begonia		O
Buxus sempervirens	box	Enteritis, may be fatal	HA
Caladium spp	taro	Burns mouth when raw	O
Calotropis gigantea	giant milkweed	Calatropin	D
Caltha palustris	marsh marigold	Protoanemonin	K
Clematis spp	traveller's joy	Protoanemonin?	K
Colocasia antiquarium	elephant ear	Burning mouth, vomiting	O
Crassula argentia	jade plant		O
Dichapetalum cymosum		Potassium fluoracetate	D
Escoecaria agallochia	blind-your-eyes		D
Hypericum spp	St John's wort	Photosensitisation	D
Impatiens noli-mi-tangere	touch-me-not		O
Lycium halimifolium	matrimony vine	Alkaloids	D
Lycopersicon esculentum	tomato	May be severe	HA
Mercurialis spp	mercury	Volatile oil	K
Philodendron spp	philodendron	Calcium oxalate	O
Piscidia erythrina	fish poison tree	Mild narcotic	D
Plumbago capensis	leadwort	May be fatal	D
Plumeria rubra	frangi-pani		D
Polyscias spp	aralias	Saponin	D
Rhododendron ponticum	rhododendron	Honey may be toxic, glycoside	N
Scrophularia aquatica	water figwort	Cardiac glycoside	N
Senecio spp	ragworts	Alkaloids	K
Trifolium hybridum	alsike clover	Photosensitisation	D
Veronia noveboracensis	ironweed	Abortifacient?	K

Part Unspecified

Anamirta spp (may = *Cocculus indicus*)		May be fatal	O
Artemesia spp	wormseed, santonin etc	May be fatal	O
Buphane spp	cape poison bulb	May be fatal	O
Caryota spp	fishtail palm		D
Cassythia filiformis	love vine	May be fatal, laurotetanine	D
Coriaria spp			D
Croton tiglium	croton	Purgative oil, may be fatal	K
Dicentra spp	bleeding heart	May be fatal	HA
Dioscorea hispida	wild yam	Dioscoreine	D
Echium vulgare	blue wood	May be fatal	O

Ervatamia coronaria	crape jasmine	Alkaloids	K
Fritillaria meleagris	fritillaria	Alkaloids?	K
Heliotropium lasiocarpine	heliotrope		D
Lophophora williamsii	peyote	Hallucinogenic	O
Lotus spp	various	May be fatal	O
Lupinus spp	lupines	May be fatal	O
Strychnos spp	strychnine plant	May be fatal	O
Tetradymia spp	rabbit bush	Photosensitisation	D
Tribulus terrestris	Devil's thorn	Photosensitisation	D

L = M. Lange and F. B. Hora; D = W. B. Deichmann and H. W. Gerarde; H = E. and H. Hvass; HA = J. W. Hardin and J. M. Arena; K = J. M. Kingsbury; N = P. North; O = S. B. O'Leary (lists some plants not in my table); Z = L. Zeitlmayr. Many plants are listed in several different texts and the selection for reference is somewhat personal.

Appendix 2 Plants causing dermatitis
(see Chapters 3 and 4)

Scientific Name	Common Name	Notes
Mechanical Injury		
Arctium lappa	burdock	Rough hairs
Bidens spp.	beggar ticks	Awned achenes
Borago officinalis	borage	Rough hairs
Corchorus capsularis	jute	Fibres may block skin glands
Cornus sanguinea	dogwood	T-shaped hairs
Echium vulgare	viper's bugloss	Rough hairs
Equisetum arvense	horsetail	Projecting silica spines
Erianthus ravennae	plume grass	Sharp edges cut skin
Hordeum vulgare	barley	Spicules on awns
Lycopsis arvensis	bugloss	Rough hairs
Opuntia microdasys	prickly pear cactus	Barbs on spicules stick firmly into skin
Oryza sativa	rice	Spicules damage skin
Pennisetum spicatum	millet	Spicules damage skin
Pentaglottis sempervirens	alkanet	Rough hairs
Pulmonaria officinalis	lungwort	Rough hairs. May also be allergenic
Stizolobium pruriens	cowhage	Barbed hairs on pods
Symphytum officinale	comfrey	Rough hairs
Verbascum thapsus	mullein	Fine hairs
Various species	algae	Spicules damage skin under water
Various species	aquatic plants	Spicules damage skin
Various species	bamboo	Spicules damage skin
Mechanical and Chemical Injury		
Arum maculatum	cuckoo pint	Tiny crystals enter skin when plant is crushed
Cnidoscolus = Jatropha	spurge nettles	Stinging hairs
Cortusa matthioli	cortusa	Details unknown
Cypripedium spp	lady's slipper orchid	May involve allergy
Hesperocnide spp	Western stinging nettle	Stinging hairs

Sparmannia africana	sparmannia	Details unknown
Ulmus procera	English elm	Details unknown
Urtica dioica	nettle	Histamine and acetyl-choline

Photosensitisers (Cause sensitivity to light)

Ammi majus	ammi	Furocoumarins present
Angelica archangelica	angelica	Furocoumarins present
Anthriscus sylvestris	cow parsley	Probably furocoumarins
Apium dulce	celery	Furocoumarins present
Citrus spp	orange, lime etc	Essential oils
Dictamnus albus	gas plant	Details unknown
Eruca sativa	rocket-salad	Effects from contact and ingestion of oil
Ficus spp	fig etc	Furocoumarins present
Heracleum mantegazzianum	giant hogweed	Furocoumarins present
Heracleum sphondylium	hogweed	Furocoumarins present
Hypericum perforatum	St John's wort	Contact or ingestion
Pastinaca sativa	wild parsnip	Furocoumarins present
Peucedanum ostruthium	masterwort	Furocoumarins present
Ruta graveolens	rue	Furocoumarins present
Thapsia garganica	thapsia	Probably furocoumarins

Allergenic Plants

Achillea millefolium	milfoil	When crushed on skin
Aconitum napellus	monkshood	Juice and contact
Argemone mexicana	Mexican poppy	Also mechanical irritation
Ailanthus altissima	tree of heaven	Leaves and flowers
Alisma plantago-aquatica	water-plantain	Tubers
Allium cepa	onion	During food preparation
Allium sativum	garlic	During food preparation
Ambrosia artemisiifolia	ragweed	Hay fever and dermatitis due to pollen
Anagallis arvensis	scarlet pimpernel	Leaves
Anthemis nobilis	chamomile	Leaves
Artemesia absinthium	wormwood	Flowers and leaves
Asparagus officinalis	asparagus	During food preparation
Atropa belladonna	deadly nightshade	Berries and sap
Berberis spp	berberis	Details unknown
Calendula officinalis	pot marigold	Leaves and sap
Caryota mitis	tufted fishtail palm	Sap
Cassia angustifolia	cassia	Leaves and sap
Catalpa speciosa	catalpa	Flowers
Caulophyllum thalictroides	blue cohosh	Berries and roots
Chimaphila umbellata	princess pine	Leaves and stem
Chlorophora excelsa	iroko	Timber and wood
Chrysanthemum cinerariifolium	insecticidal pyrethrum	Flowers and oil

C. coccineum	pyrethrum	Flowers and leaves
C. leucanthemum	marguerite	Leaves and stalks
C. maximum	shasta daisy	Flowers and leaves
C. morifolium	chrysanthemum	Flowers and leaves
C. parthenium	feverfew	Leaves
Cinnamomum zeylanicum	cinnamon	Spice, dust and oil
Cynara scolymus	globe artichoke	During food preparation
Dalbergia nigra	Rio rosewood	Wood
D. retusa	cocobolo	Wood
Daucus carota	carrot	During food preparation
Delphinium spp	larkspurs	Leaves and seeds
Derris elliptica	derris	Plant and insecticide
Dicentra spectabilis	bleeding heart	Plant
Encelia californica	encelia	Leaves
Erigeron canadensis	fleabane	Leaves and oil
Erythronium dens-canis	dog's tooth violet	Sap
Frullania spp	liverworts	On bark of timber
Gaillardia spp	gaillardia	Plant
Hedera helix	ivy	Leaves
Helenium spp	helenium	Plant
Helleborus niger	Christmas rose	Leaves
Humulus lupulus	hop	Leaves, flowers and oil
Hyacinthus orientalis	hyacinth	Bulbs and sap
Iris versicolor	iris	Rhizomes. Other species also
Iva xanthifolia	marsh elder	Leaves
Jasminum officinale	jasmine	Flowers and essential oil
Juniperus virginiana	juniper	Leaves
Khaya anthotheca	African mahogany	Wood
Leonarus cardiaca	motherwort	Leaves and oil
Lepidium sativum	garden cress	Seeds
Libocedrus decurrens	incense cedar	Wood, may be used in pencils
Linum usitatissimum	flax	Seed and linseed oil
Lycopersicon esculentum	tomato	Leaves, stem, fruit
Machaerium scleroxylon	South American rosewood	Wood
Maclura pomifera	Osage orange	Sap and spines
Mangifera indica	mango	Sap, stem and fruit peel
Mansonia altissima	mansonia	Wood
Mentzelia spp	stickleaf etc	Hairy leaves
Musa paradisiaca	banana	Pulp of banana fruit
Narcissus spp	daffodils etc	Bulbs and stems
Paratecoma peroba	white peroba	Wood
Pelargonium spp	geraniums	Plant
Phacelia spp	phacelia	Leaves
Phaseolus spp	beans	During food preparation
Philodendron scandens	philodendron	Plant
Polygonum spp	various	Leaves and sap
Polyscias spp	aralias	Plants
Primula obconica	primula	Plant. Other species rarely

Rheum spp	rhubarb	Leaves
Rumex spp	docks etc	Leaves
Sagittaria sagittifolia	arrow-head	Tubers
Sanguinaria canadensis	bloodroot	Roots and sap
Sapindus spp	soap-nut tree	Fruits
Schinus terebinthiofolius	Brazilian pepper	All parts of plant
Sedum acre	stonecrop	Sap
Semecarpus anacardium	marking-nut	Plant
Spinacia oleracea	spinach	Plant
Tagetes spp	marigolds	Plant
Tectona grandis	teak	Wood
Thuja plicata	Western red cedar	Wood
Toxicodendron spp	poison ivy etc	Plant
Trifolium hybridum	alsike clover	Leaves
Tulipa spp	tulips	Bulb and stems
Xanthium pennsylvannicum	cocklebur	Pollen and plant
Zingiber officinale	ginger	During food use
Various species	fungi	Rusts and smuts on plants
Various species	lichens	Found on logs
Various species of Pineaceae	pines etc	Wood, resins, terpentine oil

Primary Irritants

Agrimonia eupatoria	agrimony	Sap
Anacardium occidentale	cashew nut	Sap contains cardol
Ananas comosus	pineapple	Sap contains enzymes
Anemone pulsatilla	Pasque flower	Sap contains protoanemonine
Anemone nemorosa	wood anemone	Sap contains protoanemonine
Anthemis cotula	stinking mayweed	Sap
Armoracia rusticana	horseradish	Sap contains sinigrine
Brassica nigra	black mustard	Sap contains sinigrine
Bryonia dioica	white bryony	Sap
Calotropis gigantea	giant milkweed	Sap
Caltha palustris	marsh marigold	Sap
Cardiospermum halicacabum	blister creeper	Sap
Chelidonium majus	greater celandine	Sap
Clematis spp	traveller's joy etc	Sap contains protoanemonine
Cleome spp	wild mustard	Seeds and sap
Colchicum autumnale	meadow saffron	Sap
Daphne mezereum	mezereon	Sap contains mezerein
Escoecaria agallocha	blind-your-eyes	Sap
Euphorbia spp	spurges	Sap contains euphorbin
Ginko biloba	maidenhair tree	Seeds and fruit
Hippomane mancinella	manchineel tree	Sap

Hura crepitans	sandbox tree	Sap
Hyoscyamus niger	henbane	Sap and oil from plant
Lobelia spp	lobelia	Sap and leaves
Lyngbya majuscula	blue-green alga	Contact dermatitis
Monstera deliciosa	monstera	Sap
Nerium oleander	oleander	Sap
Pedilanthus tithymaloides	redbird-cactus	Milky sap
Plumbago capensis	leadwort	Sap of root and leaves
Plumeria spp	pagoda tree	Sap
Podophyllum peltatum	May apple	Sap
Ranunculus spp	buttercups etc	Sap contains protoane-monine
Raphanus sativus	radish	Sap contains sinigrine
Sapium sebiferum	Chinese tallow tree	Milky sap
Scilla spp	bluebell etc	Sap
Sisymbrium irio	London rocket	Sap from seeds

Plants Causing Dermatitis of Unproven Type

Abrus precatorius	crab's eye	Seeds
Acacia melanoxylon	black acacia	Wood
Agave americana	century plant	Plant
Allamanda cathartica	yellow allamanda	Plant
Alocasia macrorhiza	giant alocasia	Sap
Anabena spp	blue-green algae	Plant on swimmers' skin
Anthemis arvensis	corn chamomile	Plant
Aralia spinosa	devil's walking stick	Bark
Arisaema triphyllum	Jack-in-the-pulpit	Leaves and root, sap
Arnica montana	mountain tobacco	Plant and extracts
Asarum canadense	wild ginger	Leaves
Asimina triloba	pawpaw	Fruits
Brassica rapa	turnip	Plant
Buxus sempervirens	box	Leaves
Calonyction aculeatum	moonflower	Sap and vine
Campsis radicans	trumpet creeper	Leaves and flowers
Capsella bursa-pastoris	shepherd's purse	Seeds
Capsicum annuum	red pepper	Fruit and sap. Also C. frutescens
Carica papaya	papaya	Sap
Cedrus deodara	deodar	Wood, cones, sap
Cephaelis ipecacuanha	ipecac (uanha)	Plant and extracts
Chloroxylon swientenia	East Indian satinwood	Wood
Coffea arabica	coffee	Raw beans and smoke from them
Conium maculatum	poison hemlock	Leaves
Croton tiglium	purging croton	Resinous oil of plant
Cryptostegia madagascarensis	rubber vine	Plant
Cucumis sativus	cucumber	Fruit, in mouth or on skin
Datura stramonium	thorn-apple	Plant

164

Daucus carota	wild carrot	Leaves
Delphinium ajacis	larkspur	Plant
Dieffenbachia seguine	dumbcane	Leaves, plant and sap
Dirca palustris	leatherwood	Bark
Drosera spp	sundews	Crushed leaves
Fagopyrum esculentum	buckwheat	Plant
Gelsemium sempervirens	yellow jasamine	Leaves and stem
Gonioma kamassi	African boxwood	Wood
Grevillea banksii	grevillea	Plant
Guarea spp	guarea	Wood
Hibiscus esculentus	okra (lady's fingers)	During food preparation
Jatropha spp	various	Leaves and sap
Lactuca sativa	lettuce	Plant
Laportea canadensis	wood nettle	Leaves and stem, stinging hairs
Lawsonia inermis	henna	Pure extract only rarely
Melaleuca leucadendron	bottle-brush	Oil from plant
Metopium toxiferum	poison wood	Plant
Mimusop heckelii	makore	Wood
Morus rubra	red mulberry	Leaves and stem
Nicotiana tabacum	tobacco	During manufacture, leaves
Piptadenia africana	dahoma	Wood
Pithecellobium dulce	pithecellobium	Sap
Psoralea corylifolia	babchi	Seeds
Rhaphidophora aurea	hunter's robe	Sap
Rhoeo spathacea	oyster plant	Sap
Ricinus communis	castor-oil plant	Plant and seeds
Senecio confusus	Mexican flame vine	Plant
Setcreasia purpurea	purple queen	Sap
Solanum tuberosum	potato	Plant during flowering
Tamus communis	black bryony	Sap
Tanacetum vulgare	tansy	Plant
Thalictrum spp	meadow rues	Plant
Veratrum album	white hellebore	Leaves. Other species also
Vicia faba	broad bean	Pollen
Various species	grasses	Contact with leaves, pollen
Various species	woods	Contact and sawdust
Various species	pollens	Hay fever

Bibliography

Chapter 1 (The Problem and the Solution. Page 5)

Emboden Jr, W. A. *Narcotic Plants* (Macmillan, 1972)

Ghalioungui, P. *Magic and Medical Science in Ancient Egypt* (Hodder & Stoughton, 1963)

Heiser, C. B. *Nightshades, the Paradoxical Plants* (Freeman, 1969)

Mez-Mangold, L. *A History of Drugs* (Hoffman-La Roche, 1971)

Thorwald, J. *Science and Secrets of Early Medicine* (Thames & Hudson, 1962)

Chapter 2 (Plant Descriptions. Page 10)

Edible and Poisonous Fungi, Bulletin No 23 (HMSO)

Forsyth, A. A. *British Poisonous Plants*, Bulletin No 161 (HMSO)

Groves, J. W. *Edible and Poisonous Mushrooms of Canada*, Publication No 1112 of Research Branch, Canadian Dept of Agriculture, Ottawa (1962)

Hardin, J. W. and Arena, J. M. *Human Poisoning from Native and Cultivated Plants* (Duke University Press, 1969)

Hvass, E. and H. *Mushrooms and Toadstools* (Blandford, 1970)

Kingsbury, J. M. *Poisonous Plants of the U.S. and Canada* (Prentice Hall, 1964)

Lange, M. and Hora, F. B. *Collins Guide to Mushrooms and Toadstools* (Collins, 1972)

Morton, J. F. *Plants Poisonous to People in Florida and Other Warm Areas* (Hurricane House, Miami, 1971)

North, P. *Poisonous Plants and Fungi* (Blandford, 1967)

O'Leary, S. B. 'Poisoning in Man From Eating Poisonous Plants', *Archives of Environmental Health*, 9 (1964), 216–42

Zeitlmayr, L. *Wild Mushrooms: An Illustrated Handbook* (F. Muller, 1955)

Chapter 3 (Plant Poisons. Page 126)

Deichmann, W. B. and Gerarde, H. W. *Symptomatology and Therapy of Toxicological Emergencies* (Academic Press, 1964)

Dreisbach, R. H. *Handbook of Poisoning* (Lange Medical Publications, 1971)

Fowden, L., Lewis, D. and Tristram, H. 'Toxic Amino Acids', *Advances in Enzymology*, 29 (1967), 89–163

Polson, C. J. and Tattersall, R. N. *Clinical Toxicology* (Pitman, 1969)
Schultes, R. E. 'The Botanical and Chemical Distribution of Hallucinogens', *Annual Review of Plant Physiology*, 21 (1970), 571–98

Chapter 4 (Allergies. Page 136)

Adams, R. M. *Occupational Contact Dermatitis* (Lippincott Co, 1969)
Behl, P. N. *Skin-irritant and Sensitizing Plants Found in India*, (Dr. P. N. Behl, Dept of Dermatology, Irwin Hospital and M. A. Medical College, New Delhi, 1966)
Criep, L. H. *Dermatologic Allergy* (W. B. Saunders Co, 1967)
Drever, J. C. and Hunter, J. A. A. 'Giant Hogweed Dermatitis', *Scottish Medical Journal*, 15 (1971), 315–19
Hunter, D. *The Diseases of Occupations* (English Universities Press, 1969)
Rook, A. 'Plant Dermatitis – Botanical Aspects', *Transactions St John's Hospital Dermatological Society*, 46 (1961), 41–7
Schwartz, L., Tulipan, L. and Birmingham, D. J. *Occupational Diseases of the Skin* (Lea & Febiger, 1957)
Woods, B. 'Irritant Plants', *Transactions St John's Hospital Dermatological Society* (Summer 1962), 75–82

Chapter 5 (Harmful Substances in Food. Page 145)

Crosby, D. G. 'Natural Toxic Background in the Food of Man and His Animals', *Journal of Agricultural and Food Chemistry*, 17 (1969), 532–8
Food Protection Committee, 'Toxicants Occurring Naturally in Foods', National Academy of Sciences, Pub. No 1354, National Research Council (1966)
Frazier, W. C. *Food Microbiology* (McGraw-Hill, 1967)
Liener, I. E. *Toxic Constituents of Plant Foodstuffs* (Academic Press, 1969)
Mickelsen, O. and Yang, M. G. 'Naturally Occurring Toxicants in Foods', *Federation Proceedings*, 25 (1966), 104–23
Riemann, H. *Food-borne Infections and Intoxifications* (Academic Press, 1969)

General Reading

Burns, H. *Drugs, Medicine and Man* (Allen & Unwin, 1962)
Kingsbury, J. M. *Deadly Harvest* (Allen & Unwin, 1967)
Kreig, M. B. *Green Medicine* (Harrap, 1965)
Taylor, N. *Plant Drugs That Changed the World* (Allen & Unwin, 1965)

Acknowledgements

Obviously, no one person possesses a first-hand knowledge of poisoning by all the plants included in this book. My thanks are therefore due to all those doctors, botanists and other scientists whose combined efforts have contributed to the knowledge which is presented here. I also wish to thank all those, from many different places and professions, who have helped me in my task of seeking out the scattered information concerning dangerous plants, in particular staff of the herbarium and library of the British Museum (Natural History) and of the library of the Polytechnic of Central London. My special thanks are due to my editor, Emma Wood, for helping to make the complicated subject matter of this book intelligible to the ordinary reader.

Index of Common Names

Index of Scientific Names

172

174

Subject Index

176